JUMP Math

Workbook 8: Part 2

Contents

jump math

MULTIPLYING POTENTIAL.

To learn about the full range of JUMP Math publications, including pricing, discount, and ordering information, visit **www.jumpmath.org**.

If you question whether some students are capable of learning math, you will find John Mighton's books enlightening.

The Myth of Ability
Nurturing Mathematical Talent in Every Child

Mighton tells JUMP Math's fascinating story and explains its teaching method. He also provides lots of simple problems to get students started on the excitement of mastering math. *The Myth of Ability* will transform the way you look at math education.

ISBN: 978-0-88784-767-7
Published by House of Anansi Press

The End of Ignorance
Multiplying Our Human Potential

Mighton challenges us to re-examine the assumptions underlying current educational theory. He pays attention to how students pay attention, and explains why their sense of self-confidence and ability to focus are as important to their academic success as the content of their lessons.

ISBN: 978-0-676-97962-6
Published by Knopf Canada

John Mighton is the founder of JUMP Math (Junior Undiscovered Math Prodigies), an educational charity providing community and educational outreach, and professional training. He has taught at McMaster and the University of Toronto. He is an Ashoka Fellow, and an award-winning playwright.

A special thank you to Capital One Services (Canada), Inc., whose generous financial support made our Grade 7 and 8 materials possible.

JUMP Math
Toronto, Ontario
www.jumpmath.org

ISBN: 978-1-897120-33-0
Printed and bound in Canada

Writers: Dr. John Mighton, Dr. Sindi Sabourin, Huiqiu (Angela) Wang, Mary Kay Winter
Contributing writers: Margaret McClintock, Kirsten Nelson
Consultant: Dr. Melanie Tait
Cover Design: Blakeley Design
Special thanks to the design and layout team.
Cover Photograph: © Gary Blakeley, Blakeley Words+Pictures

This book is printed on 100% post-consumer waste Forest Stewardship Certified recycled paper, using plant-based inks. The paper is processed chlorine-free and manufactured using biogas energy.

*A note to educators, parents, and everyone who believes that numeracy
is as important as literacy for a fully functioning society*

Welcome to JUMP Math

Entering the world of JUMP Math means believing that every child has the capacity to be fully numerate and to love math. Founder and mathematician John Mighton has used this premise to develop his innovative teaching method. The resulting materials isolate and describe concepts so clearly and incrementally that everyone can understand them.

JUMP Math is comprised of workbooks, teacher's guides, evaluation materials, outreach programs, tutoring support through schools and community organizations, and provincial curriculum correlations.
All of this is presented on the JUMP Math website: **www.jumpmath.org**.

Read the introduction to the teacher's guide before you begin using these materials. This will ensure that you understand both the philosophy and the methodology of JUMP Math. The workbooks are designed for use by students, with adult guidance. Each student will have unique needs and it is important to provide the student with the appropriate support and encouragement as he or she works through the material.

Allow students to discover the concepts on the worksheets by themselves as much as possible. Mathematical discoveries can be made in small, incremental steps. The discovery of a new step is like untangling the parts of a puzzle. It is exciting and rewarding.

If a worksheet is marked with an…

A … then the Teacher's Guide contains activities or problem-solving lessons that you can use to introduce or reinforce the concepts on the worksheet.

E … then the Teacher's Guide contains extra questions that extend the concepts on the worksheet.

M … then the Teacher's Guide contains hints on how to teach the material on the page.

N … then students will need a notebook to answer some of the questions on the page. (We would recommend that students always have a grid paper notebook on hand, for answering extra questions and questions that require additional room.)

PA8-20: Variables

A **variable** is a letter or symbol (such as x, n, or h) that represents a number. An **algebraic expression** is a combination of one or more variables that may include numbers and operation signs.

Examples of algebraic expressions:	$5 \times T + 7$	$n \div 5$	$3z + 5y$

In the product of a number and a variable, the multiplication sign is usually dropped. For instance, $3 \times T$ is written 3T and $5 \times z + 2$ is written 5z + 2.

- -

1. It costs $3 per hour to rent a canoe.
   Write a numerical expression for the cost of renting a canoe for…

   a) 2 hours: __3 × 2__   b) 5 hours: _____

   c) 6 hours: _____   d) 7 hours: _____

2. Lei wants to go scuba diving. It costs $2 per hour to rent a wet suit.
   Write an algebraic expression for the cost of renting a wet suit for…

   a) h hours: __2 × h__ or __2h__   b) t hours: _____ or _____   c) x hours: _____ or _____

3. Write an expression for the distance a bike would travel at…

   a) Speed: 10 km per hour   b) Speed: 15 km per hour   c) Speed: 20 km per hour
      Time: 2 hours   Time: 3 hours   Time: h hours
      Distance: __10 × 2__ km   Distance: _____ km   Distance: _____ km

4. A **flat fee** (or **flat rate**) is a fixed charge that doesn't depend on how long you rent an item.

   Example: A company charges a $7 flat fee to rent a boat, plus $3 for each hour the boat is used.

   Write an expression for the amount you would pay to rent a boat for…

   a) 2 hours   b) h hours   c) t hours
      Flat fee: $9   Flat fee: $4   Flat fee: $5
      Hourly Rate: $5 per hour   Hourly Rate: $6 per hour   Hourly Rate: $4 per hour

      ___2 × 5 + 9___   _____   _____

5. Using a line, match the fee for renting a windsurf board to the correct algebraic expression:

   i)   A $15 flat fee and $7 for each hour   A: 15h + 7

   ii) $15 for each hour. No flat fee.   B: 7h + 15

   iii) A $7 flat fee and $15 for each hour.   C: 15h

6. Using n for the variable, write an expression for each cost:

		Cost ($)
a)	T-shirts are on sale for $5 each.	5n
b)	A copy shop charges 79¢ for each copy.	
c)	A rental car company charges a $15 flat fee plus $20 per day	
d)	A boat company charges a $24 flat fee plus $6 per passenger.	

PA8-21: Substitution

1. Write the number 2 in each box and find the answer:

a) $\boxed{2} + 5$

= __7__

b) $\boxed{} + 6$

= ____

c) $\boxed{} - 1$

= ____

d) $3 \times \boxed{}$

= ____

e) $7 \times \boxed{}$

= ____

f) $10 \div \boxed{}$

= ____

g) $4 \times \boxed{} + 5$

= ____

h) $5 \times \boxed{} + 3$

= ____

i) $2 \times \boxed{} - 3$

= ____

j) $8 \times \boxed{} - 15$

= ____

2. The expression 3 (7) is another form for 3×7. Write the number 2 in each bracket and evaluate:

a) 5 (2)

= __10__

b) 3 ( )

= ____

c) 4 ( )

= ____

d) 7 ( )

= ____

e) 10 ( )

= ____

3. A company charges a $6 flat rate to rent a pair of skis plus $3 for each hour you use the skis. This fee is given by the expression: 3h + 6. Find the cost of renting the skis for…

a) 4 hours

3 (4) + 6

= 12 + 6

= 18

b) 2 hours

c) 5 hours

d) 7 hours

4. Replace the variable with the given value and evaluate (this is called <u>substitution</u>):

a) 5h + 2, h = 3

5 (3) + 2

= 15 + 2

= 17

b) 2n + 3, n = 6

c) 5t – 2, t = 4

Answer the remaining questions in your notebook.

d) 3m + 9, m = 8

e) 9 – 2z, z = 4

f) 5n – 3n + 2, n = 5

5. Pizza slices cost $3 and drinks $2. The cost of **p** pizza slices and **d** drinks is: 3p + 2d. Find the cost of the following amounts:

a) 5 pizza slices and 4 drinks

b) 6 pizza slices and 6 drinks

c) 2 pizza slices and 7 drinks

6. The area of a triangle is given by $A = \frac{1}{2} \times b \times h$ (also written $A = \frac{1}{2}bh$), where b = base and h = height. Evaluate the expression for the area of a triangle with:

a) b = 2   h = 5

b) b = 7   h = 8

c) b = 15   h = 10

jump math
MULTIPLYING POTENTIAL.

E

Patterns & Algebra 2

TEACHER: Review the concept of direct variation in section PA8-12. In the patterns in Question 1 below the number of blocks varies directly with the figure number.

1. i)   Write an expression that shows how to calculate the number of blocks from the Figure Number.
    ii) Using the letter n to stand for the Figure Number, write an algebraic expression for the total number of blocks in each sequence:

    NOTE: In mathematics, the expression 3 × n is traditionally written in short form as 3n.

a)

Figure 1   Figure 2   Figure 3

   i)   _____4 × Figure Number_____
   ii) _____4n_____

b)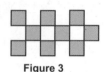

Figure 1   Figure 2   Figure 3

   i)   _____
   ii) _____

c)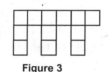

Figure 1   Figure 2   Figure 3

   i)   _____
   ii) _____

d)

Figure 1   Figure 2   Figure 3

   i)   _____
   ii) _____

2. In each pattern below, the number of *shaded* blocks increases directly with the Figure Number. The *total* number of blocks however <u>does not</u> increase directly.

    i)   Write a rule for the number of shaded blocks in each sequence.

    ii) Write a rule for the *total* number of blocks in each sequence.

    iii) Using n for the figure number, write an algebraic expression for the total number of blocks.

a)

Figure 1   Figure 2   Figure 3

   i)   _____3 × Figure Number_____
   ii) _____3 × Figure Number + 1_____
   iii) _____3n + 1_____

b)

Figure 1   Figure 2   Figure 3

   i)   _____
   ii) _____
   iii) _____

Answer the remaining questions in your notebook.

c)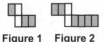

Figure 1 Figure 2   Figure 3

d)

Figure 1 Figure 2 Figure 3

e)

Figure 1   Figure 2   Figure 3

(continued)

3. Tom wants to find an algebraic expression for each term in the sequence 3, 7, 11, 15, …

Step 1: He makes a chart to show the term number (n), and the product of n times the gap.

Term Number (n)	n × GAP	Term
1	1 × 4 = 4	3
2	2 × 4 = 8	7
3	3 × 4 = 12	11

gap
4
4

Step 2: He writes a rule and an algebraic expression for the chart.

Term Number (n)	n × GAP	Term
1	1 × 4 = 4	3
2	2 × 4 = 8	7
3	3 × 4 = 12	11

Rule: $4 \times$ Term Number $- 1$
Algebraic Expression: $4n - 1$

Find a rule and algebraic expression (using n for the term number) for the following sequences.

a)

Term Number (n)	n × GAP	Term
1		2
2		7
3		12
4		17

Rule: _____

Algebraic Expression:

b)

Term Number (n)	n × GAP	Term
1		1
2		4
3		7
4		10

Rule: _____

Algebraic Expression:

Answer the remaining parts for Question 3 in your notebook.

c) 3, 5, 7, 9   d) 9, 20, 31, 42   e) 17, 27, 37, 47

f) 12, 15, 18, 21   g) 2, 14, 26, 38   h) 53, 55, 57, 59

4. i) Write a sequence of numbers that gives the number of blocks of toothpicks in each figure.
    ii) Write an algebraic expression for the number of blocks or toothpicks in each figure.

a)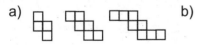

    i) <u>4, 6, 8</u>
    ii) <u>2n + 2</u>

b)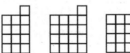

    i) _____
    ii) _____

c)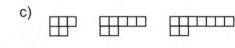

    i) _____
    ii) _____

d)

    i) _____
    ii) _____

e)

    i) _____
    ii) _____

f)

    i) _____
    ii) _____

Answer the following questions in your notebook.

1. A store charges $5 each hour to rent a pair of skates. Write an expression (using h to stand for hours) for the cost of renting the skates.

2. Write an expression that gives the total amount each company would charge for a boat carrying **n** people on a whale-watching tour.

Prices for a Whale-Watching Tour

	Company A	Company B	Company C
Rental fee for boat	$100	$120	$70
Fee for each life jacket	$3	$5	$7

3. Write an expression for the perimeter of each shape (**x** stands for the length of the unknown sides):

a)

b)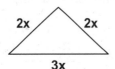

c)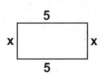

d)

4. Claire has $63 in savings. She earns $6 an hour.
   Write an expression for the total amount she will have saved after working h hours.

5. Using the letters A for area, P for perimeter, l for length, w for width, b for base and h for height, write an expression to represent each statement:

   a) The area of a rectangle is equal to its length times its width.

   b) The area of a parallelogram is equal to its base times its height.

   c) The area of a triangle is half its base times its height.

   d) The perimeter of a rectangle is twice the sum of its length and width.

6. Tom wants to find the 10th term in the sequence 3, 7, 11, 15, …

Term Number (n)	n × GAP	Term
1	1 × 4 = 4	3
2	2 × 4 = 8	7
3	3 × 4 = 12	11

He makes a chart and writes a rule for his chart.

Rule: 4n – 1

From his rule he can see the value of the 10th term is:

4 × (10) – 1 = 40 – 1 = 39.

Find a rule (using n for the term number) for the following sequences. Then find the value of the tenth term for each sequence:

a) 4, 9, 14, 19

b) 4, 10, 16, 22

c) 3, 9, 15, 21

d) 5, 16, 27, 38

e) 11, 21, 31 , 41

f) 13, 15, 17, 19

g) 3, 10, 17, 24

h) 44, 47, 50, 53

7.
```
            A
        B       B
      C     C       C
    D     D     D     D
  E     E     E     E     E
```

If the pattern continues, how many letters will appear in the "K" row?

HINT: Write a sequence for the number of letters in each row, then write a rule for the sequence.

PA8-24: Equations

1. Find the number that makes each equation true (by guessing and checking) and write it in the box.

   a) $\boxed{} + 5 = 9$

   b) $\boxed{} + 4 = 8$

   c) $\boxed{} + 2 = 8$

   d) $10 - \boxed{} = 4$

   e) $15 - \boxed{} = 12$

   f) $12 - \boxed{} = 10$

   g) $3 \times \boxed{} = 6$

   h) $4 \times \boxed{} = 20$

   i) $3 \times \boxed{} = 15$

   j) $\boxed{} \div 3 = 4$

   k) $\boxed{} \div 5 = 4$

   l) $\boxed{} \div 2 = 12$

   m) $6 + 2 = 4 + \boxed{}$

   n) $12 - 8 = \boxed{} + 5$

   o) $\boxed{} + \boxed{} + 2 = 8$

2. Find a set of numbers that makes each equation true. (Some questions have more than one answer.) **NOTE: In a given question, congruent shapes must represent the <u>same</u> number.**

   a) $\square + \square + \bigcirc = 8$

   b) $\square + \square + \bigcirc = 12$

   c) $\diamondsuit + \diamondsuit + \bigcirc + \bigcirc = 8$

   d) $\square + \triangle + \bigcirc = 7$

3. Find two different answers for the equation:

   a) $\square + \square + \bigcirc = 5$

   b) $\square + \square + \bigcirc = 5$

Show your work for the remaining questions in your notebook.

4. How many answers can you find for the equation $\square + \square + \bigcirc = 9$?

5.   Eric threw 3 darts and scored 8 points.
   The dart in the centre ring is worth more than the others.
   Each dart in the outer ring is worth more than one point.
   How much is each dart worth?
   HINT: How can an equation like the one in 2 a) help you solve the problem?

6. Eric threw 4 darts and scored 16 points. The rings are worth more points as they get closer to the centre. The dart in the inner-most ring is worth twice as much as each dart in the outer-most ring. How much is each dart worth?

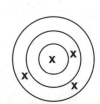

jump math
MULTIPLYING POTENTIAL.

E   **Patterns & Algebra 2**

1. Solve each equation by inspection. Guess and check:

   a) $\boxed{} + 5 = 18$ b) $3 \times \boxed{} = 27$ c) $\boxed{} \div 5 = 3$ d) $\boxed{} - 4 = 14$

   e) $12 - \boxed{} = 10$ f) $\boxed{} \times 6 = 18$ g) $12 + \boxed{} = 20$ h) $24 \div \boxed{} = 8$

2. What number does the letter represent?

   a) $x + 3 = 9$ b) $A - 3 = 5$ c) $n + 5 = 11$ d) $6x = 18$ e) $y + 5 = 17$

   $x =$ $A =$ $n =$ $x =$ $y =$

   f) $3n = 15$ g) $b \div 2 = 8$ h) $4x = 20$ i) $z - 2 = 23$ j) $m - 2 = 25$

   $n =$ $b =$ $x =$ $z =$ $m =$

BONUS

3. What number does the box or the letter "n" represent? Guess and check:

   a) $3 \times \boxed{} + 2 = 8$ b) $3 \times \boxed{} + 4 = 10$ c) $5 \times \boxed{} - 2 = 13$

   $\boxed{} =$ $\boxed{} =$ $\boxed{} =$

   d) $4 \times \boxed{} - 1 = 15$ e) $6 \times \boxed{} - 5 = 31$ f) $7 \times \boxed{} - 2 = 19$

   $\boxed{} =$ $\boxed{} =$ $\boxed{} =$

   g) $2 \times \boxed{} + 3 = 9$ h) $5 \times \boxed{} - 2 = 8$ i) $3 \times \boxed{} + 5 = 14$

   $\boxed{} =$ $\boxed{} =$ $\boxed{} =$

   j) $2 \times \boxed{} - 5 = 3$ k) $7 \times \boxed{} + 2 = 16$ l) $n + 5 = 4 + 10$

   $\boxed{} =$ $\boxed{} =$ $n =$

   m) $n - 2 = 12 - 4$ n) $4n + 1 = 13$ o) $5n + 2 = 27$

   $n =$ $n =$ $n =$

   p) $5 = 3n + 2$ q) $11 = 4n - 1$ r) $17 - 3 = 2n - 4$

   $n =$ $n =$ $n =$

To solve the equation x + 2 = 7, Chloe thinks:

"If x + 2 = 7, I can add 2 to x to make 7   but <u>then</u>   I can subtract 2 from 7 to make x"

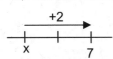 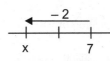

If x + 2 = 7	then	x = 7 − 2

1. Rewrite each equation to show how you would work backwards. Draw an arrow as in a):

a) If x + 2 = 5   then   x = 5 − 2

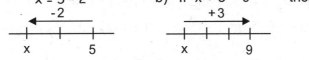

b) If x + 3 = 9   then &underline{\qquad}

 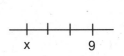

c) If x + 4 = 8   then &underline{\qquad}

d) If x + 5 = 7   then &underline{\qquad}

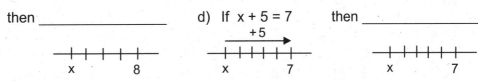 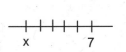

2. Solve each equation by working backwards. Show all your steps as in a):

a) x + 4 = 10   b) x + 2 = 6   c) x + 2 = 9   d) x + 4 = 5   e) x + 6 = 10

x = 10 − 4

x = 6

To solve the equation x − 3 = 2, Stan thinks:

"If x − 3 = 2, I can subtract 3 from x to make 2   but <u>then</u>   I can add 3 to 2 to make x."

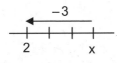 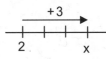

If x − 3 = 2	then	x = 2 + 3

3. Rewrite each equation to show how you would work backwards. Draw an arrow as in a):

a) If x - 4 = 3   then &underline{\qquad}

b) If x - 2 = 9   then &underline{\qquad}

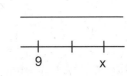

4. Solve each equation by working backwards. Show all your steps as in a):

a) x − 2 = 10   b) x − 3 = 7   c) x − 5 = 8   d) x − 6 = 9   e) x − 4 = 12

x = 10 + 2

x = 12

STUDENT: In algebra, a multiplication sign between a number and a variable is usually dropped:

$3 \times T$ is written $3T$ $P \times 2$ is written $2P$

As well, division is often written in fractional form: $T \div 4$ is written $\frac{T}{4}$ $x \div 6$ is written $\frac{x}{6}$

To solve the equation $3x = 6$, Jill thinks: "If $3x = 12$, I can multiply x by 3 to get 12. But <u>then</u> I can divide 12 by 3 to find x."

If $3x = 12$ <u>then</u> $x = \frac{12}{3}$

5. Solve the following equations by working backwards as in a):

a) $3x = 12$ b) $2x = 10$ c) $4x = 12$ d) $2x = 14$ e) $3x = 21$

    $x = \frac{12}{3}$

    $x = 4$

f) $7x = 28$ g) $6x = 18$ h) $7x = 49$ i) $8x = 48$ j) $9x = 72$

6. Solve each equation by working backwards. Show all your steps:

a) $x + 2 = 9$ b) $x - 3 = 11$ c) $3x = 9$ d) $8x = 32$ e) $x - 4 = 17$

BONUS:

f) $x - .5 = .7$ g) $x + .5 = .8$ h) $x + .35 = .71$ i) $x + 325 = 587$

j) $x - 286 = 793$ k) $x + 3 + 2 = 10$ l) $x + 5 - 2 = 13$ m) $x + 7 - 4 = 20 + 3$

Answer the remaining questions in your notebook.

7. How can you solve the equation $\frac{x}{3} = 4$ by working backwards?

8. Write as many multiplication and division statements as you can that are **equivalent** to the given statement:

a) $12 \div 3 = 4$ b) $A\,B = C$ c) $\frac{X}{Y} = Z$

PA8-27: Two-Step Problems

The expression 3 × 2 is short for 2 + 2 + 2. Similarly, 3x is short for x + x + x.

1. Each bag contains the same number of apples. Write a mathematical expression for the total number of apples, letting x stand for the number of apples in one bag:

a) x + 2

b) _____

c) _____

d) _____

e) _____

2. In an **equation**, two quantities are compared with an equal sign. In each question below…
   i) Write an expression for the total number of apples.
   ii) Write an **equation** by setting the expression you created in part i) equal to the total number of apples.

a) There are **7 apples** in total.

   Expression:

   x + 2

   Equation:

   x + 2 = 7

b) There are **7 apples** in total.

   Expression:

   _____

   Equation:

   _____

c) There are **15 apples** in total.

   Expression:

   _____

   Equation:

   _____

d) There are **12 apples** in total.

   Expression:

   _____

   Equation:

   _____

e) There are **14 apples** in total.

Expression:

_____

Equation:

_____

f) There are **18 apples** in total.

Expression:

_____

Equation:

_____

Answer the remaining questions in your notebook.

3. From the information given in Question 2, determine how many apples are in each bag. Explain your reasoning in two cases.

4. Farad has 3 bags of apples plus 2 extra apples. He has 11 apples altogether. Alana finds the number of apples in each bag by working backwards:

	Alana's reasoning	Alana's equation
= 11		$3x + 2 = 11$
= 9	There are two apples outside the bags so there are $11 - 2$ apples inside the bags.	$3x = 11 - 2$ $3x = 9$
= 3	There are 9 apples in 3 bags so there are $9 \div 3 = 3$ apples in each bag.	$x = \frac{9}{3}$ $x = 3$

5. Write an equation and find the number of apples in each bag by working backwards:

a) 10 apples in total

b) 13 apples in total

c) 17 apples in total

PA8-28: More Two-Step Problems

1. To solve the question 3x + 2 = 17, Miguel works backwards:

   "If 3x + 2 = 17 then I can **add** 2 to 3x to get 17   but **then**   I can **subtract** 2 from 17 to get 3x, so 3x = 17 – 2."

   Use Miguel's reasoning to complete each statement:

   a) If 5x + 2 = 22   then __5x = 22 - 2__

      so __5x = 20__

   b) If 3x + 1 = 7   then _____

      so _____

   c) If 4x + 5 = 13   then _____

      so _____

   d) If 2x + 6 = 18   then _____

      so _____

   e) If x + 7 = 15   then _____

      so _____

   f) If 6x + 2 = 26   then _____

      so _____

   g) If 3x + 5 = 14   then _____

      so _____

   h) If 5x + 8 = 58   then _____

      so _____

Answer the remaining questions in your notebook.

2. Work backwards to solve each equation. Show all your steps as in a):

   a) 4x + 3 = 11

      4x = 11 - 3

      4x = 8

      x = $\frac{8}{4}$

      x = 2

   b) 5x + 3 = 28

   c) 3x + 5 = 17

   d) 2x + 27 = 43

   e) 6x + 7 = 19

   f) 3x + 4 = 37

   g) 23z + 5 = 51

   h) 11x + 34 = 100

   i) 43x + 21 = 150

3.
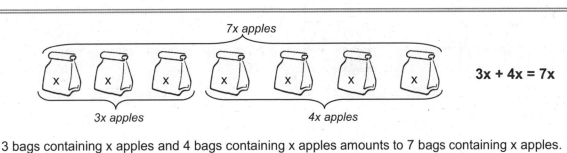

   3 bags containing x apples and 4 bags containing x apples amounts to 7 bags containing x apples.

   Use this way of adding shown above to solve the following in your notebook:

   a) 2x + 5x = 21   b) 5x + 4x + 2 = 20   c) 6x + x + 4 = 32   d) 3x + 2x + 2 = 22

4. Each container holds an equal number of marbles. Write and solve an equation to find the number of marbles in each container. If there are…

   a) 17 marbles altogether.   b) 41 marbles altogether.   c) 65 marbles altogether.

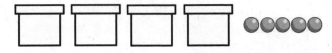

Patterns & Algebra 2

1. In each diagram below, the blocks have the same mass. Find the mass of each block by first writing an equation (use the letter given to represent the mass of blocks). All measurements are in grams:

a)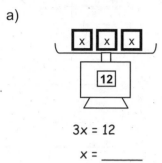

$3x = 12$

$x =$ _____

b)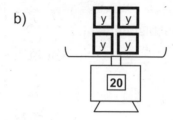

c)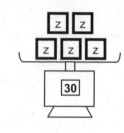

2. ➢ Write an equation for each diagram.
    ➢ Then remove the same mass of blocks from each side (so that only blocks with mass x are left on the left hand balance).
    ➢ Then show what mass would be subtracted from each side of the equation and solve the equation.
    The first one is done for you:

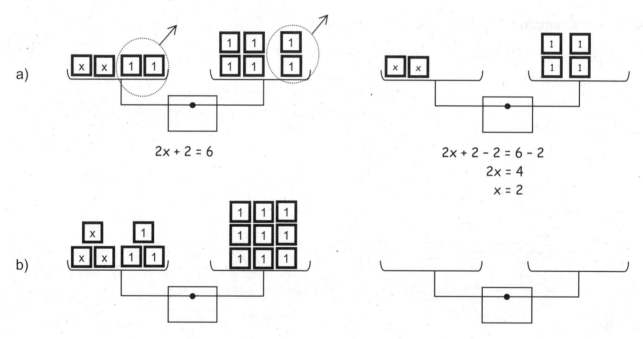

a)

$2x + 2 = 6$

$2x + 2 - 2 = 6 - 2$
$2x = 4$
$x = 2$

b)

Answer the remaining questions in your notebook.

3. Draw a balance as in Question 2 to represent each question. Show how many blocks you would remove from each side of the balance:

a) $3x + 2 = 11$ b) $5x + 3 = 13$ c) $2x + 5 = 9$

PA8-30: Advanced Algebra

1. For each pattern below write…

   i) A <u>sequence</u> giving the number of blocks in each figure.
   ii) A <u>rule</u> for the pattern.
   iii) An <u>algebraic expression</u> for the number of blocks in the nth figure.
   iv) An <u>equation</u> that tells you which figure would have 33 blocks. Then solve the equation.

   a)

   Figure 1   Figure 2   Figure 3

   b)

   Figure 1   Figure 2   Figure 3

   i) _____5, 7, 9_____   i) _____

   ii) ____2 × Figure Number + 3____   ii) _____

   iii) ____2n + 3____   iii) _____

   iv)   2n + 3 = 33   iv)
            2n = 33 - 3
            2n = 30
             n = 15

   The 15th figure would have 33 blocks.

   Answer the remaining questions in your notebook.

   c)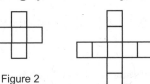

   Figure 1

   Figure 2

   Figure 3

   d)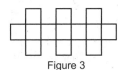

   Figure 1   Figure 2   Figure 3

2. For each sequence below…

   i) Write an algebraic expression for the nth term of the sequence.
   ii) Find the term number for the term that has a value of 50. (Is it the 4th term? The 5th term?....etc.)
   HINT: Write an equation in which you set the expression you found in part i) to be equal to 50.

   a) 10, 15, 20, 25   b) 8, 15, 22, 29   c) 10, 14, 18, 22

3. A company charges a flat fee of $2 plus $3 each hour to rent a pair of rollerblades:

   a) Write an expression for the cost of renting the rollerblades for h hours.
   b) If you had $26, how long could you rent the rollerblades for?

4. Carol has $48 in savings. She earns $9 an hour:

   a) Write an equation for the amount she would have after working for h hours.
   b) Find how many hours she would have to work if she wants to buy a jacket that costs…

      i) $84.   ii) $138.   iii) $228.

5. A phone company charges an $8 flat fee plus 10¢ per minute for phone service. How many minutes could you talk if you had...

   a) $12?   b) $15?   c) $20?

jump math
MULTIPLYING POTENTIAL

Patterns & Algebra 2

6. To solve word problems, it helps to turn words into algebraic expressions:

Clues that you need to **add**:	"increased by"	"sum"	"more than"	
Clues that you need to **subtract**:	"less than"	"difference"	"decreased by"	"reduced by"
Clues that you need to **multiply**:	"product"	"times"	"twice as many"	
Clues that you need to **divide**:	"divided by"	"divided into"		

Match up each algebraic expression with the correct phrase:

2 more than a number	4x	2 divided into a number	3x
A number divided by 3	x − 2	a number reduced by 4	x ÷ 2
2 less than a number	x + 2	a number times 3	x + 3
the product of a number and 4	x − 3	twice as many as a number	x − 4
a number decreased by 3	x ÷ 3	a number increased by 3	2x

7. Write an algebraic expression for each sentence:

   a) Four more than a number.   b) A number decreased by 10.   c) The product of 7 and a number.

   d) The sum of a number and 7.   e) Two less than a number.   f) A number divided by 8.

   g) A number increased by 9.   h) A number reduced by 4.   i) The product of a number and 3.

   j) Five times a number.   k) 6 divided into a number.   l) Twice as many as a number.

8. Solve the following problems by first writing an equation:
   NOTE: The word "is" translates to "=" so "Two more than a number is seven" can be written x + 2 = 7.

   a)   Four more than a number is eighteen.   b)   Five less than a number is 12.

   c)   Five times a number is thirty.   d)   Six times a number is forty two.

   e)   A number multiplied by two then increased   f)   A number multiplied by three then decreased
        by five is thirty five.   by four is seventeen.

9. Write an expression for the perimeter of each figure. Which figure in each sequence would have perimeter 66?

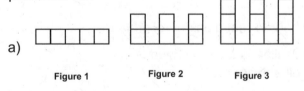

a)

Figure 1   Figure 2   Figure 3

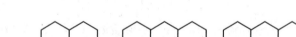
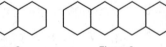

b)

Figure 1   Figure 2   Figure 3

10. The fence around a trapezoidal field has perimeter 800 m. Find x.

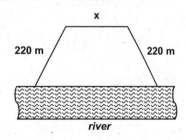

x

220 m   220 m

river

11. The perimeter of the field is 1400 m. Find x.

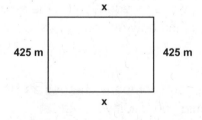

x

425 m   425 m

x

E   Patterns & Algebra 2

PA8-31: Graphs

1. For each set of points, write a list of ordered pairs, and then complete the T-table:

a)

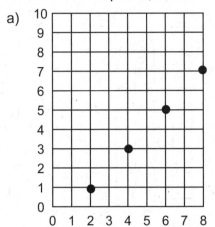

Ordered Pairs	First Number	Second Number
(2 , 1)	2	1
(,)		
(,)		
(,)		

b)

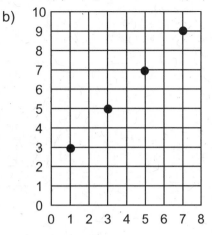

Ordered Pairs	First Number	Second Number
(,)		
(,)		
(,)		
(,)		

c)

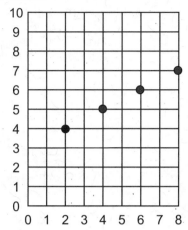

Ordered Pairs	First Number	Second Number
(,)		
(,)		
(,)		
(,)		

2. Mark 4 points on the line segments. Then write a list of ordered pairs, and complete the T-table:

a)

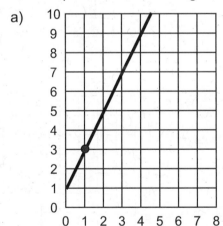

Ordered Pairs	First Number	Second Number
(1 , 3)	1	3
(,)		
(,)		
(,)		

b)

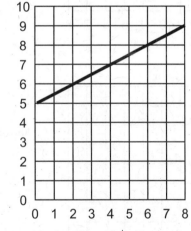

Ordered Pairs	First Number	Second Number
(,)		
(,)		
(,)		
(,)		

c)

Ordered Pairs	First Number	Second Number
(,)		
(,)		
(,)		
(,)		

3. Write a list of ordered pairs based on the T-table provided. Plot the ordered pairs and connect the points to form a line:

First Number	Second Number
3	1
4	3
5	5
6	7

(,)

(,)

(,)

(,)

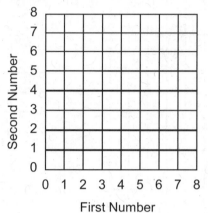

4. Draw a graph for each T-table (as in Question 1):
    HINT: **Make sure you look carefully at the scales in c) and d).**

a)

Input	Output
2	5
4	6
6	7
8	8

b)

Input	Output
1	7
2	6
3	5
4	4

BONUS:

c)

Input	Output
2	4
4	8
6	12
8	16

d)

Input	Output
1	6
3	8
5	10
7	12

5. Draw a coordinate grid on grid paper and plot the following ordered pairs:
    (1,2), (3,5), (5,8), and (7,11).

6. On grid paper, make a T-table and graph for the following rules:
    a) Multiply by 2 and subtract 1.
    b) Multiply by 4 and subtract 3.
    c) Divide by 2 and add 3.

7. Make a T-table for each set of points on the coordinate grid. Then, write a rule for each T-table:

Graph A

Input	Output

Graph B

Input	Output

Graph C

Input	Output

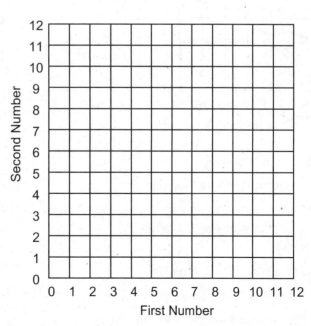

Rule for Table A: _____

Rule for Table B: _____

Rule for Table C: _____

8. Mark <u>four</u> points that lie on a straight line in the coordinate grid. Then, make a T-table for your set of points:

First Number	Second Number

Answer these questions in your notebook.

1.

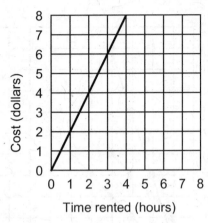

The graph shows the cost of renting a pair of skates.

a)   If you rented skates for 2 hours, how much would you pay?

b)   How much does the cost rise every hour?

c)   How much would you pay to skate for 5 hours?

d)   If you paid 6 dollars, how long would you be able to skate for?

e)   How much would you pay to skate for 30 min?

2.

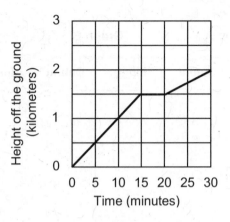

To reach the top of a ski mountain, Kathy takes two different chairlifts.

a)   How high did the first chairlift take her?

b)   How high off the ground will Kathy start skiing?

c)   How long did it take Kathy to switch between chairlifts? How do you know?

d)   Did the two chairlifts travel at the same speed?

3.

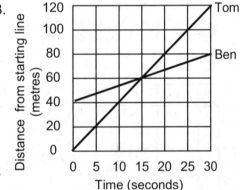

Ben and Tom run a 120 m race.

a)   How far from the start was Tom after 10 seconds?

b)   How far from the start was Ben after 15 seconds?

c)   Who won the race? By how much?

d)   How much of a head start did Ben have?

e)   How many seconds from the start did Tom overtake Ben?

4.

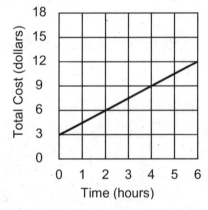

The graph shows the cost of renting a bike from Mike's store.

a)   How much would you pay to rent the bike for…
     i) 2 hours   ii) 4 hours   iii) 3 hours

b)   How much do you pay for the bike before you have even ridden it?

c)   Dave's store charges $3.00 an hour for a bike. Whose store would you rent from if you wanted the bike for 3 hours?

PA8-33: Using Graphs to Investigate Patterns

1. Use the graph to find the missing values in the sequence:

a)
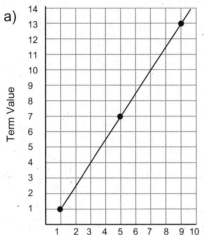

Term Number	Term Value
1	1
3	
5	7
	10
9	13

b)
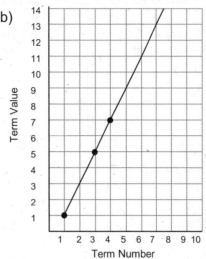

Term Number	Term Value
1	1
	3
3	5
4	7
5	

2. Extend the line to find the value of the 11th term:

a)
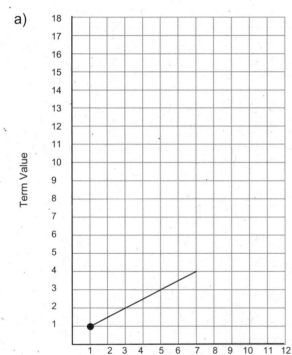

Value of the 11th term _____

b)

Value of the 11th term _____

Answer the remaining questions in your notebook.

3. For each sequence below make a table of values that matches the term number and the term value. Draw a graph for your table and extend the graph to find the value of the 7th term:

a) 2, 5, 8, 11   b) 1, 3, 5, 7

4. Draw a graph to show how many toothpicks would be needed for the 8th figure:

a)      b)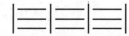

Patterns & Algebra 2

PA8-34: Discovering Relations

1. Write a rule that relates the numbers in columns 1 (C1) and 2 (C2), to those in column 3 (C3):

    HINT: The rule will involve adding or subtracting the columns. The first one is done for you.

a)

C1	C2	C3
3	7	4
4	10	6
5	6	1

Rule: Subtract C1 from C2

b)

C1	C2	C3
7	4	3
2	1	1
5	3	2

Rule:

c)

C1	C2	C3
3	3	6
4	5	9
5	7	12

Rule:

d)

C1	C2	C3
9	13	4
1	5	4
3	6	3

Rule:

e)

C1	C2	C3
8	2	10
5	10	15
10	4	14

Rule:

f)

C1	C2	C3
15	3	18
25	5	30
17	7	24

Rule:

Answer the remaining questions in your notebook.

2. Write a rule that relates the numbers in columns 1 and 2 (C1, C2) to those in column 3 (C3):

    HINT: The rule will involve multiplying or dividing the columns.

a)

C1	C2	C3
1	4	4
2	5	10
3	6	18

b)

C1	C2	C3
3	12	4
10	50	5
8	16	2

c)

C1	C2	C3
6	1	6
9	3	3
21	3	7

d)

C1	C2	C3
16	8	2
24	6	4
32	4	8

3. Write a rule that relates the numbers in columns 1 and 2 to those in column 3:

    HINT: The rule will involve adding, subtracting, multiplying or dividing the columns and then adding or subtracting a fixed number. (For example: "Add column 1 and column 2, then add 7.")

a)

C1	C2	C3
1	3	9
2	7	14
3	4	12

b)

C1	C2	C3
2	3	3
4	4	6
6	5	9

c)

C1	C2	C3
3	2	7
6	1	7
4	3	13

d)

C1	C2	C3
7	2	9
10	6	8
2	1	5

e)

C1	C2	C3
0	5	2
2	10	9
5	14	16

f)

C1	C2	C3
1	4	7
2	11	25
3	5	18

g)

C1	C2	C3
4	1	5
12	5	9
13	9	6

h)

C1	C2	C3
4	2	3
8	4	3
12	3	5

PA8-34: Discovering Relations (continued)

4. Write the length of the base and the height of each parallelogram in the chart. Then find the area of the parallelogram by counting squares and half squares.

   Write a rule relating the base and the height of the parallelogram:

   TEACHER:
   If your students need practice finding the area by counting half squares, assign or review section ME8-21.

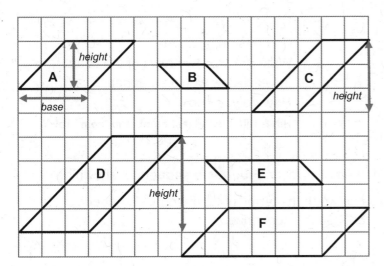

	Base	Height	Area
A			
B			
C			
D			
E			
F			

RULE:

5. Leonard Euler, the famous mathematician, discovered a rule relating the number of faces and vertices in a 3-D shape to the number of edges in the shape.

   Fill in the chart and see if you can discover the rule yourself!

   TEACHER: For a review of 3-D shapes and nets, see G8-47 to G8-50.

3-D Shape	# of Faces	# of Vertices	# of Edges		3-D Shape	# of Faces	# of Vertices	# of Edges
a) Triangular Pyramid				b) Triangular Prism			
c) Square-based Pyramid				d) Pentagonal Prism			
e) Cube				f) Hexagonal Prism			

jump math
MULTIPLYING POTENTIAL.

Patterns & Algebra 2

Answer the following questions in your notebook.

1. The average temperature on the earth's surface is about 15°C. The temperature increases .03° C for every metre you go down in the earth's crust. What is the average temperature 1 km below the surface?

2.
```
              1
          2   3   4
        5   6   7   8   9
     10  11  12  13  14  15  16
```

   a) Describe any patterns you see in the rows and columns of the chart.
   b) Write the next two rows of the chart.
   c) In which row would 99 appear? How do you know?

   HINT: What is the last number in the nth row?

3. One of the most famous sequences in mathematics is the **Fibonacci sequence**, shown below:

   a) In the circles provided, write the steps between the terms of the Fibonacci sequence. Then use the pattern in the steps to continue the sequence:

   1 , 1 , 2 , 3 , 5 , 8 , 13 , 21 , _____ , _____

   b) Which numbers in the Fibonacci sequence are odd? Which ones are even?

   c) Add the first four odd Fibonacci numbers. Then add the first two even numbers. Add the first six odd Fibonacci numbers. Then add the first three even numbers. What do you notice?

   d) Is the 38th term in the Fibonacci sequence even or odd? Explain.

4. For each sequence below:
   i) Write an expression for the nth term
   ii) Find the 11th term.
   iii) Find the term number of the term that has value 39.

   a) 3, 9, 15, 21...   b) 9, 14, 19, 24...   c) 7, 11, 15, 19...   d) 4, 11, 18, 25...

5. The perimeter of each figure is 42 m. How long is each side?

   a) 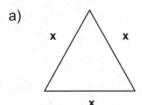   b) 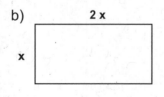   c)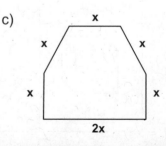

NS8-47: Introduction to Ratios

A **ratio** is a comparison of two or more numbers. A ratio of two numbers may be written in three different ways.

The ratio of squares to triangles is 2 to 3   2 : 3 $\frac{2}{3}$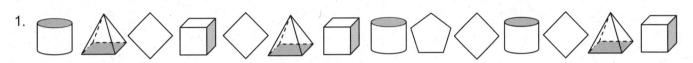

When there are more than two numbers, the colon (:) notation is more general than fractions because fractions cannot be used to compare three numbers. The ratio of circles to squares to triangles is 2 : 2 : 3.

1.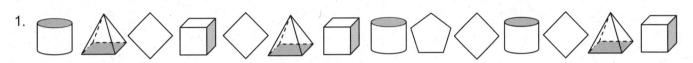

   a) The ratio of pyramids to cubes is _____ : _____   b) The ratio of diamonds to pentagons is ____ : ____

   c) The ratio of cylinders to diamonds to pyramids is _____ : _____ : _____

2. Write ratios to represent the following:

    a) The total number of days in a week to the number of days in the weekend __7__ : __2__

    b) The total number of days in a week to the number of days in October _____ : _____

3. Write the number of vowels compared to the number of consonants in the following words:

    a) apple _2_ : _3_   b) banana ___ : ___   c) orange ___ : ___   d) grape ___ : ___

4. Write the ratio of the lengths:

    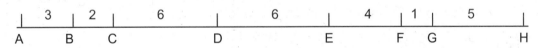

    a) AB to CD _____ : _____   b) BC to DE _____ : _____   c) EF to FH _____ : _____

    d) EF to BC to FG _____ : _____ : _____   e) AB to GH to CD _____ : _____ : _____

5. To make punch, you need 4 L of ginger ale, 2 L of orange juice, and 3 L of mango juice. What is the ratio of ginger ale to punch?

    _____

6. a) What does the ratio 2 : 5 describe?

    _____

    b) What does the ratio 3 : 10 describe?

    _____

A recipe for granola calls for 2 cups of raisins for every 3 cups of oats. To find out how many cups of raisins she will need for 12 cups of oats, Eschi writes a sequence of **equivalent ratios**. (She multiplies both terms in the ratio 2 : 3 by 2, then by 3, then by 4.)

$$2:3 = 4:6 = 6:9 = 8:12$$

---

1. Starting with the given ratios, write a sequence of four ratios that are all equivalent.

   a) $2:5 = 4:10 = \quad : \quad = \quad :$ b) $3:4 = \quad : \quad = \quad : \quad = \quad :$

   c) $4:9 =$ d) $5:7 =$

2. a) 4 cm on a map represents 30 km. How many km do 12 cm on the map represent?

   b) Four bus tickets cost $5.50. How much will 16 tickets cost?

   c) A math test has 3 geometry questions for every 8 algebra questions. How many algebra questions are on a test with 9 geometry questions?

3. Falmataa plants 3 rows of vegetables in $\frac{1}{2}$ an hour. He wants to know how many rows of vegetables he can plant in 6 hours.

   He changes the ratio $\frac{1}{2}:3$ to a more convenient form by doubling both terms of the ratio:

$\frac{1}{2}$ hour : 3 walls = 1 hour : 6 walls
1 hour : 6 walls = 6 hours : 36 walls

   Then, he multiplies each term by 6.

   Change each ratio so the number on the left is a whole number:

   a) $\frac{1}{2}$ hour : 3 km ran =

   b) $\frac{1}{3}$ cup of flour : 3 cups of milk =

   c) $\frac{1}{4}$ hour : 5 km rowed =

   HINT: For the ratios below, multiply each term by 10.

   d) .4 cup of raisins : 3 cups of oats =

   e) .3 litre of gas used : 6 km =

   f) 1.9 : .4   g) $\frac{3}{10} : \frac{2}{5}$ h) .9 : .2 : .3

4. In your notebook, solve each problem by changing the ratio into a more convenient form.

   a) Rhonda can ride her bike 4 km in $\frac{1}{4}$ of an hour. How far can she ride in 5 hours?

   b) A recipe for 12 cookies uses $\frac{1}{2}$ cup pecans and 1 cup of sugar. Angela has 3 cups of pecans. How much sugar will she need? How many cookies can she make?

NS8-49: Finding Equivalent Ratios

> There are 3 boys for every 2 girls in a class of 20 children. To find out how many boys are in the class, write out a sequence of ratios. Stop when the terms of the ratio add to 20:
>
> 3 boys : 2 girls = 6 boys : 4 girls = 9 boys : 6 girls = 12 boys : 8 girls
>
> 12 boys + 8 girls = 20 kids. So there are 12 boys in the class.

1. Write a sequence of ratios to solve each problem. The first one is started for you.

   a) There are 5 boys for every 4 girls in a class of 27 children. How many girls are in the class?

   $5 : 4 = 10 : 8 =$

   b) There are 2 red marbles for every 7 blue marbles in a box. With 27 marbles, how many marbles are blue?

   c) A recipe for punch calls for 3 L of orange juice for every 4 L of mango juice. How many litres of orange juice are needed to make 21 L of punch?

> 5 subway tickets cost \$4. Kyle wants to know how much 20 tickets will cost. He writes the ratio of tickets to dollars as a fraction. Then, he finds an equivalent fraction by multiplying:
>
> **Step 1:** $\dfrac{4}{5} = \dfrac{?}{20}$
>
> **Step 2:** $\dfrac{4}{5} \overset{\times 4}{\underset{\times 4}{=}} \dfrac{}{20}$
>
> **Step 3:** $\dfrac{4}{5} \overset{\times 4}{\underset{\times 4}{=}} \dfrac{16}{20}$

2. Solve the following ratios. Draw arrows to show what you multiply by.

   a) $\dfrac{3}{4} \overset{\times 5}{\underset{\times 5}{=}} \dfrac{}{20}$
   b) $\dfrac{1}{5} = \dfrac{}{15}$
   c) $\dfrac{3}{5} = \dfrac{}{35}$
   d) $\dfrac{4}{7} = \dfrac{}{49}$

   e) $\dfrac{3}{8} = \dfrac{}{24}$
   f) $\dfrac{2}{3} = \dfrac{}{18}$
   g) $\dfrac{13}{20} = \dfrac{}{100}$
   h) $\dfrac{5}{9} = \dfrac{}{72}$

BONUS: **NOTE: Sometimes, the arrow may point from right to left.**

3. a) $\dfrac{15}{} \overset{\times 5}{\underset{\times 5}{=}} \dfrac{3}{4}$
   b) $\dfrac{12}{} = \dfrac{2}{5}$
   c) $\dfrac{15}{} = \dfrac{3}{7}$
   d) $\dfrac{12}{18} = \dfrac{}{3}$

4. For each question below, you will have to reduce the fraction given before you can find the equivalent fraction. The first one has been started for you:

   a) $\dfrac{8}{10} = \dfrac{4}{5} = \dfrac{}{15}$
   b) $\dfrac{4}{6} = \dfrac{}{} = \dfrac{}{15}$
   c) $\dfrac{40}{100} = \dfrac{}{} = \dfrac{}{45}$

   d) $\dfrac{15}{18} = \dfrac{}{} = \dfrac{}{30}$
   e) $\dfrac{70}{100} = \dfrac{}{} = \dfrac{}{90}$
   f) $\dfrac{50}{75} = \dfrac{}{} = \dfrac{}{36}$

jump math
MULTIPLYING POTENTIAL.

Number Sense 2

NS8-50: Word Problems

There are 3 cats in a pet shop for every 2 dogs. If there are 12 cats in the shop, how many dogs are there?

Solution:

Step 1:
Write, as a fraction, the ratio of the two things being compared: $\frac{3}{2}$

Step 2:
Write, in words, what each number stands for:
cats $\frac{3}{2}$
dogs

Step 3:
On the other side of an equals sign, write the *same* words, on the *same* levels:

cats $\frac{3}{2}$ = ——— cats
dogs   dogs

Step 4:
Re-read the question to determine which quantity (i.e. number of cats or dogs) has been given (in this case, cats) – then place that quantity on the proper level:

cats $\frac{3}{2}$ = $\frac{12}{}$ cats
dogs   dogs

Step 5:
Solve the ratio.

Solve the following questions in your notebook.

1. A zoo has 3 tigers for every 4 lions.
    If there are 12 lions in the zoo, how many tigers are there?

2. A list of numbers has 3 primes for every 5 composites.
    If the list has 12 primes, how many composites does it have?

3. Four bus tickets cost $7. How many bus tickets can you buy with $21?

4. An unusual deck of cards has 4 face cards for every 7 numbered cards.
    If the deck has 16 face cards, how many numbered cards does it have?

5. A basketball team won 3 out of every 5 games they played.
    They played a total of 15 games. How many games did they win?

    NOTE: The quantities are "games won" and "games played."

6. Three cm on a map represent 7 km in real life. If a lake is 35 km long,
    how long would it be on the map? (Here the quantities compared are cm and km).

7. A zoo has 2 mammals for every 3 reptiles and 5 birds.
    If the zoo has 12 mammals, how many reptiles and birds does it have?
    HINT: First compare mammals to reptiles and then compare mammals to birds.

MULTIPLYING POTENTIAL.

Number Sense 2

NS8-51: Further Ratios

1. Express each of the ratios below in **lowest terms** by dividing each term in the ratio by the same number:

   a) $2^{\div 2} : 6^{\div 2}$
   $= 1 : 3$

   b) $4 \quad : 6$

   c) $10 \quad : 15$

   d) $12 \quad : 18$

   e) $27 \quad : 36$

Answer the questions below in your notebook.

2. Find the missing term in each expression by first reducing the ratio on the left to lowest terms:

   a) $25 : 20 = 10 : \square$

   b) $24 : 21 = 8 : \square$

   c) $12 : 8 = 33 : \square$

   d) $18 : 15 = 24 : \square$

3. Express each of the ratios in lowest terms by dividing each term in the ratio by the same number.
   a) $10 : 12 : 14$

   b) $10 : 25 : 30$

   c) $6 : 15 : 21$

4. The ratio of uncooked to cooked rice is $2 : 5$. How much uncooked rice would you need to make 50 g of cooked rice? To make 320 mL of cooked rice?

5. The ratio of girls to boys in a class is $2 : 3$. There are 12 boys in the class.

   a) How many students are in the class?   b) Write the ratio of girls to students in lowest terms.

6. In a scale diagram, the **scale** tells you the ratio of any dimension of the diagram to the corresponding dimension of the object.

   diagram A
   scale: $\frac{1}{30}$

   a) Measure the diagram of the monkey. The scale indicates that 1 cm in the diagram is equivalent to _____ cm in real life.

   b) Use a ratio to find its actual height.

7. Write a ratio to find each missing term:
   NOTE: When the numerator of a scale is larger than the denominator, the drawing is larger than the actual object.

Scale	Length in Diagram	Length in Real Life
$\frac{1}{5}$	16 cm	
$\frac{1}{6}$		54 m
$\frac{7}{1}$	14 cm	

8. Find the distances between the following cities on the map and in real life:

   Scale:
   0   100 km

   London   Amsterdam

   Brussels

   Paris

	On map	Real
Paris – Brussels		
London – Amsterdam		
London – Paris		

E   **Number Sense 2**

A **rate** is a comparison of two quantities measured in different units. For instance, speed is a rate, as it compares the number of km traveled to the number of hours spent traveling.

1. Find the missing numbers by first drawing arrows as in a):

   a) $\dfrac{10 \text{ km}}{2 \text{ h}} \xrightarrow[\div 2]{\div 2} \dfrac{5 \text{ km}}{1 \text{ h}}$

   b) $\dfrac{18 \text{ km}}{3 \text{ h}} = \dfrac{\text{km}}{1 \text{ h}}$

   c) $\dfrac{20 \text{ m}}{8 \text{ s}} = \dfrac{\text{m}}{2 \text{ s}}$

   d) $\dfrac{100 \text{ mg}}{20 \text{ mL}} = \dfrac{20 \text{ mg}}{\text{mL}}$

   e) $\dfrac{\$35}{7 \text{ kg}} = \dfrac{\$5}{\text{kg}}$

   f) $\dfrac{\$5.50}{10 \text{ min}} = \dfrac{\$}{2 \text{ min}}$

   g) $\dfrac{\$96}{6 \text{ h}} = \dfrac{\$32}{\text{h}}$

   h) $\dfrac{50 \text{ kg}}{20 \text{ L}} = \dfrac{\text{kg}}{4 \text{ L}}$

Answer the remaining questions in your notebook.

2. Find the missing numbers by first writing each ratio in fraction form:

   a) $40 : 8 = 5 : \boxed{}$

   b) $72 : 18 = \boxed{} : 3$

   c) $54 : 9 = \boxed{} : 6$

   d) $66 : \boxed{} = 44 : 4$

   In a **unit rate** one of the terms is equal to one.

3. Find the unit rate for each rate by reducing the ratio to lowest terms (include the units):

   a) $20 \text{ km} : 5 \text{ h} = \boxed{} : 1 \text{ h}$ b) $60¢ : 3 \text{ apples} = \boxed{} : 1 \text{ apple}$ c) $\$30 : 2 \text{ h} = \boxed{} : 1 \text{ h}$

   d) $96 \text{ m} : 12 \text{ s} = \boxed{} : 1 \text{ s}$ e) $\$80 : 16 \text{ jar} = \boxed{} : 1 \text{ jar}$ f) $\$68 : 4 \text{ kg} = \boxed{} : 1 \text{ kg}$

4. Solve each problem by first changing the rate to a unit rate:
   a) Dana rode 60 km in 5 hours. How far could she ride in 8 hours?
   b) Cindy can type 60 words in 3 min. How many words can she type in 5 minutes?
   c) If 45 miles per hour is 20 m/s, how fast is 72 miles per hour in m/s?

5. Change both prices to a unit rate to find out which offer is a better buy.
   a) $1.40 for 7 peaches or $ 1.00 for 4 peaches.
   b) 66¢ for 3 lemons or 85¢ for 5 lemons.
   c) $3.39 for 3 tennis balls or $4.20 for 4 tennis balls?

6. Clare can cycle at a speed of 23 km/hr. Erin can cycle at a speed of 17 km/hr. How much further can Clare cycle in 3 hours than Erin?

7. a) A car travels 45 kilometres in half an hour. What is its average speed in km/hr?
   b) A cheetah runs 700 metres in 30 seconds. What is its average speed in km/hr?

8. Karen walked at a speed of 4 km/hr. At this rate, how far can she walk in

   a) 2 hr   b) $\frac{1}{2}$ hr   c) 15 minutes

9 Estimate to the nearest half hour how long it would take to drive:

   a) 254 km   b) 723 km   c) 1425 km

Maximum
Speed
100 km/h

NS8-53: Percents

A **percent** is a ratio that compares a number to 100. The term "percent" means "out of 100" or "for every 100." For instance, 84% on a test means 84 out of 100.

You can think of percent as a short form for a fraction with 100 in the denominator:

Example: $45\% = \frac{45}{100}$

----

1. Write the following percents as fractions:

   a) 17%   b) 34%   c) 10%   d) 29%

   e) 45%   f) 100%   g) 1%   h) 80%

2. Write the following fractions as percents:

   a) $\frac{50}{100}$ b) $\frac{46}{100}$ c) $\frac{62}{100}$ d) $\frac{100}{100}$

   e) $\frac{25}{100}$ f) $\frac{99}{100}$ g) $\frac{90}{100}$ h) $\frac{1}{100}$

3. Write the following decimals as percents, by first turning them into fractions. The first one has been done for you:

   a) $.72 = \frac{72}{100} = 72\%$ b) .54   c) .09

4. Write the fraction as a percent by changing it to a fraction over 100. The first one has been done for you:

   a) $\frac{3 \times 20}{5 \times 20} = \frac{60}{100} = 60\%$ b) $\frac{4}{5}$

   c) $\frac{5}{5}$ d) $\frac{9}{10}$

   e) $\frac{3}{4}$ f) $\frac{1}{2}$

   g) $\frac{1}{10}$ h) $\frac{3}{20}$

   i) $\frac{13}{20}$ j) $\frac{8}{25}$

   k) $\frac{18}{25}$ l) $\frac{24}{25}$

   m) $\frac{37}{50}$ n) $\frac{43}{50}$

jump math
MULTIPLYING POTENTIAL.

Number Sense 2

NS8-53: Percents *(continued)*

5. Write the following decimals as percents. The first one has been done for you:

   a) $.2 = \dfrac{2}{10} \dfrac{\times 10}{\times 10} = \dfrac{20}{100} = 20\%$

   b) $.3$

   c) $.4$

   d) $.8$

6. What percent of the figure is shaded?

   a)

   b)

   c)

   d)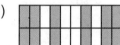

7. Change the following fractions to percents by first reducing them to lowest terms:

   a) $\dfrac{9}{15} \dfrac{\div 3}{\div 3} = \dfrac{3}{5} = \dfrac{3}{5} \dfrac{\times 20}{\times 20} = \dfrac{60}{100} = 60\%$

   b) $\dfrac{3}{15}$

   c) $\dfrac{9}{18}$

   d) $\dfrac{6}{24}$

   e) $\dfrac{24}{32}$

   f) $\dfrac{36}{45}$

   g) $\dfrac{24}{60}$

   h) $\dfrac{22}{40}$

   i) $\dfrac{32}{80}$

   j) $\dfrac{28}{56}$

   k) $\dfrac{75}{150}$

   l) $\dfrac{60}{75}$

NS8-54: Visual Representations of Percents

1. Fill in the chart below. The first one has been done for you:

Drawing				
Fraction	$\frac{23}{100}$	$\frac{}{100}$	$\frac{35}{100}$	$\frac{}{100}$
Decimal	0.23	0.__ __	0.__ __	0.39
Percent	23%	74%	____ %	____ %

2. Shade 50% of each box:

   a)

   b)

3. Colour 50% of the rectangle blue, 30% red, and 20% green:

4. Write a fraction for each part shaded. Then write the fraction with a denominator of 100. Then write a decimal and a percent for each:

   a)  Fraction ____

   Fraction with denominator 100 ____

   decimal _____ percent _____

   b) Fraction ____

   Fraction with denominator 100 ____

   decimal _____ percent _____

5. Extend each line segment to show 100%:

   a) 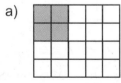 | 50% |

   b) | 20% |

   c) | 20% |

   d) | 75% |

   e)  0%   60%

   f) 0%   80%

   g)  0%   30%

   h) 0%   50%

1. Write < or > or = between the following pairs of numbers. First change each pair of numbers to a pair of fractions with the same denominator. The first one is done for you:

a)

$\frac{1}{2}$	47%
$\frac{50 \times 1}{50 \times 2}$	$\frac{47}{100}$
$\frac{50}{100}$ >	$\frac{47}{100}$

b)

$\frac{1}{2}$	49%

c)

$\frac{3}{5}$	66%

d)

.37	73%

e)

.02	20%

f)

$\frac{1}{10}$	10%

g)

$\frac{19}{20}$	98%

h)

$\frac{27}{50}$	54%

i)

.9	9%

j)

$\frac{17}{25}$	68%

k)

$\frac{13}{20}$	65%

l)

.42	40%

2. Complete the charts:

Fraction	Decimal	Percent
$\frac{2}{5}$		
	.75	
$\frac{11}{20}$		
		70%

Fraction	Decimal	Percent
	.30	
$\frac{12}{16}$		
		25%
	.85	

3. In your notebook, write each set of numbers in order from least to greatest, by first changing each number to a fraction:

a) $\frac{1}{5}$, 22% , .15

b) $\frac{1}{4}$, .50 , 43%

c) $\frac{1}{10}$, .01 , 15%

d) $\frac{2}{3}$, 60% , .57

E **Number Sense 2**

If you use a thousands cube to represent 1 whole, you can see that taking $\frac{1}{10}$ of a number is the same as dividing by 10 (the decimal shifts one place left):

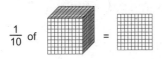

$\frac{1}{10}$ of [cube] = [flat] $\frac{1}{10}$ of [flat] = [rod] $\frac{1}{10}$ of [rod] = [cube unit]

$\frac{1}{10}$ of 1 = .1 $\frac{1}{10}$ of .1 = .01 $\frac{1}{10}$ of .01 = .001

---

1. Find $\frac{1}{10}$ of the following numbers by shifting the decimal. Write your answers in the boxes provided:

   a) 7   b) 10   c) 35   d) 210   e) 6.4   f) 50.6

2. 10% is short for $\frac{10}{100}$ or $\frac{1}{10}$. Find 10% of the following numbers:

   a) 1   b) 3.9   c) 4.05   d) 6.74   e) .09   f) 60.08

3. You can find percents that are multiples of 10 as follows:

   Example: Finding 30% of 21 is the same as finding 10% of 21 and multiplying the result by 3:

   Step 1 10% of 21 = $\boxed{2.1}$

   Step 2 3 × $\boxed{2.1}$ = 6.3   So 30% of 21 = 6.3.

   Find the percents using the method above:

   a) 30% of 15   b) 50% of 24   c) 20% of 7.8

   i) 10% of __15__ = [ ]   i) 10% of _____ = [ ]   i) 10% of _____ = [ ]

   ii) 3 × [ ] = _____   ii) ___ × [ ] = _____   ii) ___ × [ ] = ___

   d) 40% of 75   e) 90% of 86   f) 80% of .5

   i) 10% of ___ = [ ]   i) 10% of _____ = [ ]   i) 10% of ___ = [ ]

   ii) ___ × [ ] = _____   ii) ___ × [ ] = _____   ii) ___ × [ ] = ___

35% is short for $\frac{35}{100}$. To find 35% of 27, Sadie finds $\frac{35}{100}$ of 27.

Step 1   She multiplies 27 by 35.

	2	3
	2	7
x	3	5
1	3	5
8	1	0
9	4	5

Step 2   She divides the result by 100.

945 ÷ 100 = 9.45

So 35% of 27 is 9.45.

---

1. Find the following percents using Sadie's method:

   a)   **25% of 44**

   Step 1:

   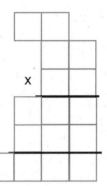

   Step 2:

   _____ ÷ 100 =

   So _____ of _____ is _____.

   b)   **18% of 92**

   Step 1:

   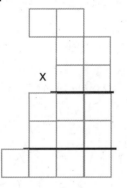

   Step 2:

   _____ ÷ 100 =

   So _____ of _____ is _____.

Answer the following questions in your notebook.

2. Find the following percents using Sadie's method:

   a) 23% of 23   b) 15% of 26   c) 26% of 15   d) 64% of 58

   e) 58% of 64   f) 50% of 81   g) 81% of 50   h) 92% of 11

3. 25% is equal to $\frac{1}{4}$ and 75% is equal to $\frac{3}{4}$. Find:

   a) 25% of 80   b) 25% of 28   c) 25% of 156   d) 75% of 60   e) 75% of 244

Answer the questions below in your notebook.

1. Fill in the following chart. The first one is done for you:

Item	Regular Price	Percent Discount	Discount	Sale Price
Gloves	$36.00	10%	$ 3.60	36.00 – 3.60 = 32.40
Shoes	$49.92	25%		
CD	$14.90	30%		

2. 3 is what percent of 20? You can find out by writing a ratio. Write a ratio to answer the following questions:

   HINT: You will have to reduce some ratios.

   The part goes here $\longrightarrow \dfrac{3}{20} = \dfrac{?}{100} \implies \dfrac{3}{20} = \dfrac{15}{100}$
   The whole goes here $\nearrow$
   So 3 is 15% of 20.

   a) 5 is what percent of 25?   b) 17 is what percent of 20?   c) 4 is what percent of 5?

   d) 7 is what percent of 14?   e) 16 is what percent of 48?   f) What percent of 20 is 13?

3. Students in a class were asked to choose one sport to participate in for a sports day:

   a) Complete the chart.

   b) How many students are in the class?

Sport	Fraction of Class that chose the sport	Percent	Decimal	Number of Students that chose the sport
Soccer	$\frac{1}{5}$	20%	0.2	4
Swimming	$\frac{2}{5}$	40 %	0.4	8
Baseball	$\frac{1}{4} \times 50$	25%	.25	5
Gymnastics	$\frac{3}{20}$	15%	.15	3

20

4. Find each amount by using a ratio or decimal multiplication:

   a) What is 22% of 70?   b) What is15% of 9?   c) What percent of 50 is 10?

   d) What percent of 20 is 9?   e) What percent of 25 is 6?   f) What is 18% of 42%?

5. Grasslands make up 2.5% of the habitat of birds in North America; 2.5% is short for $\dfrac{2.5}{100}$.

   If you multiply the numerator and denominator by 10, you get a proper fraction: $\dfrac{2.5 \times 10}{100 \times 10} = \dfrac{25}{1000} = \dfrac{1}{40}$

   Express each percent as a proper fraction and reduce to lowest terms:

   a) 17.5%   b) .7%   c) 6.4%   d) .04%

6. a) Change the following decimals to percents:

   i) .235 = $\dfrac{235}{1000} = \dfrac{235 \div 10}{1000 \div 10} = \dfrac{23.5}{100}$ = 23.5%   ii) .273   iii) .848   iv) .369

   b) Change the following fractions to decimals by long division. Express your answers as percents:

   i) $\frac{7}{20}$ ii) $\frac{11}{20}$ iii) $\frac{3}{8}$ iv) $\frac{5}{8}$

7. After a 10% discount, a book costs $27.00. How much does the book cost without the discount?

1. Write the number of girls (**g**), boys (**b**), and children (**c**) in each class:

   a) There are 8 boys and 5 girls in a class: **b:** _____ **g:** _____ **c:** _____

   b) There are 4 boys and 7 girls in a class: **b:** _____ **g:** _____ **c:** _____

   c) There are 12 boys and 15 girls in a class: **b:** _____ **g:** _____ **c:** _____

   d) There are 9 girls in a class of 20 children: **b:** _____ **g:** _____ **c:** _____

2. Write the number of boys, girls and children in each class.

   Then write the fraction of children who are boys and the fraction who are girls in the boxes provided:

   a) There are 5 boys and 6 girls in a class.   **b:** ____ ⬚ **g:** ____ ⬚ **c:** ____

   b) There are 15 children in the class. 8 are boys.   **b:** ____ ⬚ **g:** ____ ⬚ **c:** ____

Answer the remaining questions in your notebook.

3. Write the fraction of children in the class who are boys and the fraction who are girls:

   a) There are 5 boys and 12 children in the class.   b) There are 3 boys and 2 girls in the class.

   c) There are 9 girls and 20 children in the class.   d) The ratio of boys to girls is 5:9 in the class.

   e) The ratio of girls to boys is 7:8 in the class.   f) The ratio of boys to girls is 10:11 in the class.

4. From the information given, determine the number of girls and boys in each class:

   a) There are 20 children in a class. $\frac{2}{5}$ are boys.   b) There are 42 children. $\frac{3}{7}$ are girls.

   c) There are 15 children. The ratio of girls to boys is 3:2.

   d) There are 24 children. The ratio of girls to boys is 3:5.

5. Find the number of boys and girls in each classroom:

   a) In classroom A, there are 25 children: 60% are girls.

   b) In classroom B, there are 28 children. The ratio of boys to girls is 3 : 4.

6. For each question below, say which classroom has more girls:

   a) In classroom A, there are 40 children. 60% are girls.

   In classroom B, there are 36 children. The ratio of boys to girls is 5 : 4.

   b) In classroom A, there are 28 children. The ratio of boys to girls is 5 : 2.

   In classroom B, there are 30 children. $\frac{3}{5}$ of the children are boys.

7. In the word "Whitehorse"...

   a) ... what is the ratio of vowels to consonants?   b) ... what fraction of the letters are vowels?

   c) ... what percent of the letters are consonants?

NS8-60: Further Fractions and Percents

1. Write each fraction as an equivalent fraction over 100 and then as a percent:

   a) $\dfrac{3}{10} = \dfrac{}{100} = $ ___%

   b) $\dfrac{12}{30} = \dfrac{}{10} = \dfrac{}{100} = $ ___ %

   c) $\dfrac{33}{75} = \dfrac{}{25} = \dfrac{}{100} = $ ___ %

   d) $\dfrac{7}{25} = \dfrac{}{100} = $ ___%

   e) $\dfrac{9}{20} = \dfrac{}{100} = $ ___%

   f) $\dfrac{52}{80} = \dfrac{}{20} = \dfrac{}{100} = $ ___%

2. To find the percent of 360 that 72 represents, follow the steps below:

Step 1	**Step 2**	**Step 3**	**Step 4**
Write 72 as a fraction of 360:	Compare this fraction to a fraction with a denominator of 100:	Reduce $\dfrac{72}{360}$ to lowest terms:	Solve:
$\dfrac{72}{360}$	$\dfrac{72}{360} = \dfrac{}{100}$	$\dfrac{1}{5} = \dfrac{}{100}$	$\begin{array}{c}\times 20\\ \dfrac{1}{5} \Rightarrow \dfrac{20}{100}\\ \times 20\end{array}$ So, 72 is 20% of 360.

   Answer the following questions. Show your rough work in your notebook:

   a) 270° is ____ % of 360°.   b) 18° is ____ % of 360°.   c) 288° is ____ % of 360°.

3. To find the percents below, using the method of section NS8-57:

   a) ____° is 60% of 360°.   b) ____° is 20% of 360°.   c) ____° is 10% of 360°.

   d) ____° is 85% of 360°.   e) ____° is 50% of 360°.   f) ____° is 45% of 360°.

4. Complete each chart and then use your protractor to draw a circle graph. Make sure it is clear which part of the circle represents which choice:

   a) Survey Results: Daily Newspaper Habit   Title: _____

	Percent	Angle in Circle
delivered to home	40%	$\dfrac{40}{100} \times 360° = 144°$
buy occasionally	50%	
never look at	10%	

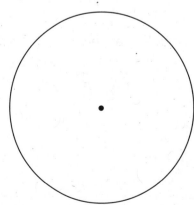

Number Sense 2

b)   Survey Results: How Students Spend Money   Title: _____

	Percent	Angle in Circle
entertainment	45%	
personal care	30%	
snacks	10%	
savings	15%	

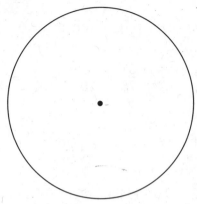

5.   Complete the relative frequency charts. Then draw a circle graph in your notebook:

a)

Favourite Sport	Frequency	Fraction of total	Percent
Hockey	8	$\frac{8}{20}$	40%
Swimming	5		
Running	4		
Other	3		

b)

Favourite Type of Game	Frequency	Fraction of total	Percent
Board game	11		
Card game	1		
Video game	24		
Other	314		

6.   A percent can be larger than 100. For example, to find 150% of 30, multiply 30 by 150, then divide the result by 100: $30 \times 150 = 4500$, so 150% of 30 is $4500 \div 100 = 45$.

a)   _____ is 23% of 40   b)   _____ is 200% of 15   c)   _____ is 150% of 22

d)   _____ is 100% of 30   e)   _____ is 180% of 35   f)   _____ is 250% of 100

g)   _____ is 275% of 32   h)   _____ is 112.5% of 200

HINT: 112.5% $= \frac{112.5}{100} = \frac{1125}{1000}$

7.   To find what percent of 60 that 90 represents, compare $\frac{90}{60}$ to a fraction over 100:

$\frac{90}{60} = \frac{?}{100}$ $\xrightarrow{reduce}$ $\frac{3}{2} = \frac{}{100}$ $\longrightarrow$ $\frac{3 \times 50}{2 \times 50} = \frac{150}{100}$, so 90 is 150% of 60.

a)   80 is _____ % of 40   b)   75 is _____% of 60   c)   99 is _____% of 44

d)   45 is _____% of 15   e)   75 is _____% of 50   f)   55 is _____% of 40

HINT: Compare to a fraction over 1000 before comparing to a fraction over 100.

If you perform the operations in the expression $8 \div 2 \div 2$ in different orders you get different answers:

$$8 \div 2 \div 2 = 4 \div 2 = 2 \qquad\qquad 8 \div 2 \div 2 = 8 \div 1 = 8$$

Divide first   Divide first

To avoid confusion, mathematicians established a standard **order for operations**:

(1) First perform all operations inside **B**rackets
(2) Then calculate **E**xponents
(3) Then **D**ivide and **M**ultiply in order from left to right
(4) Then **A**dd and **S**ubtract in order from left to right

B rackets
E xponents
D ivide and
M ultiply
A dd and
S ubtract

Answer the remaining questions in your notebook.

1. Perform the following calculations using the correct order of operations:

> *Example:*
> $4 \times 3 \div 2$
> $= 12 \div 2$
> $= 6$
>
> $8 + 4 \div 2 - 7$
> $= 10 - 7$
> $= 3$
>
> $4 \times (8 - 2)$
> $= 4 \times 6$
> $= 24$

a) $3 \times 4 \times 2$

b) $18 \div 3 \div 2$

c) $9 \times 2 \div 6 \times 7$

d) $10 \times 4 \div 2 \div 5$

e) $6 \times 2 - 3$

f) $6 - 2 \times 3$

g) $20 \div 4 + 2$

h) $20 + 4 \div 2$

i) $2 + 4 \times 6 - 5$

j) $6 + 12 \div 3 - 7$

k) $4 \times 3 \div 6 + 5$

l) $5 \times 7 - 10 \div 2$

m) $4 \div (2 - 1)$

n) $(5 - 1) \times 3$

o) $20 - (14 - 7)$

p) $(12 - 4) \div 4$

q) $(12 - 3) \times 8 \div 4$

r) $4 \times 3 - (6 + 5)$

s) $(5 + 3) \times (2 + 4)$

t) $(24 - 2 \times 6) \div 4$

BONUS: u) $(24 - (2 + 4)) \div 3$

2. Exponents are performed immediately after brackets:

> *Examples:* $(5 + 2)^2 = 7^2 = 49$ $3^{2+2} \div 3 = 3^4 \div 3 = 81 \div 3 = 27$ $4^{(5+3) \div 4} = 4^{8 \div 4} = 4^2 = 16$

Evaluate:

a) $7 + 6^2$

b) $128 \div 8^2$

c) $(17 + 13) \div 5^2$

d) $17 - 13 - 2^2$

e) $3^2 + 2^2$

f) $(3 + 2)^2$

g) $3^2 + 4 \times 5$

h) $2^{(4+2) \div 2}$

i) $2^{4+2} \div 2$

3. Add brackets where necessary to the following equations to make them true:

a) $6 - 2 \times 3 = 12$

b) $16 \div 2 \times 2 = 4$

c) $3 + 1 \times 7 - 2 = 20$

d) $3 + 1 \times 7 - 2 = 26$

e) $3 + 1 \times 7 - 2 = 8$

f) $8 - 4 \times 2 + 5 = 28$

g) $8 - 4 \times 2 + 5 = 13$

h) $2 + 5^2 = 49$

i) $5^{4 - 2 + 1} = 5$

j) $12 \div 2^2 = 36$

k) $3^3 \div 3 + 6 = 3$

l) $3^3 \div 3 + 6 = 15$

BONUS: m) $34 - 5 + 2 \div 3 = 9$

4. Translate the words into expressions and evaluate:

> *Example:*   Add 8 and 3. Then subtract 4. Then multiply by 3.   <u>Answer:</u> $(8 + 3 - 4) \times 3 = 21$

a) Multiply 6 and 5.
Then subtract 3.
Then add 5.

b) Subtract 6 from 9.
Then multiply by 2.
Then add 4.

c) Divide 4 by 2.
Then add 10.
Then subtract 4.

d) Divide 6 by 3.
Then add 5.
Then subtract 3.

5. Write the following expressions in words: *Example:* $7 - 2 \times 3$ <u>Answer:</u> Multiply 2 and 3. Subtract from 7.

a) $(6 + 1) \times 2$

b) $4 \times (3 - 1 + 5)$

c) $(3 - 2) \times (4 + 17)$

d) $3 \times (7 - (4 + 2))$

NS8-62: Square Roots

> The **square root** of a number *n* is a number you can multiply by itself to get the number *n*:
> For instance, the square root of 25 is 5 since 5 × 5 = 25. The square root of 25 is written $\sqrt{25}$.

1. Fill in the missing numbers:

    a) 36 = <u>6</u> × <u>6</u>   b) 9 = __ × __   c) 16 = __ × __   d) 49 = __ × __   e) 64 = __ × __

    so $\sqrt{36}$ = <u>6</u>   so $\sqrt{9}$ = ___   so $\sqrt{16}$ = ___   so $\sqrt{49}$ = ___   so $\sqrt{64}$ = ___

2. Each side of a square with area *n* has length $\sqrt{n}$. Draw a square with the given area. Then write the side length as a square root of the area of the square:

    a)   area 4   b)   area 9   c)   area 16

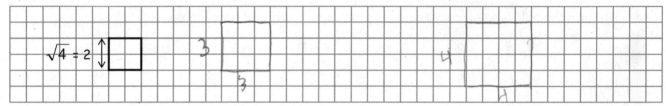

3. Fill in the missing numbers:

    a) $\sqrt{\boxed{}}$ = 5   b) $\sqrt{100}$ = $\boxed{}$ c) $\sqrt{\boxed{}}$ = 9   d) $\sqrt{1}$ = $\boxed{}$

4. Use the pattern to find the missing numbers:

    $\sqrt{100}$ = <u>10</u> $\sqrt{10000}$ = <u>100</u> $\sqrt{1000000}$ = _____ $\sqrt{100000000}$ = _____

5. The shaded square in part a) below has area 10 square units. So the side length is $\sqrt{10}$. You can see from the picture that $\sqrt{10}$ lies between the whole numbers 3 and 4. Fill in the missing numbers in parts b) and c):

    a)   b)   c)

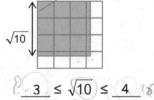 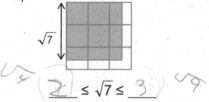 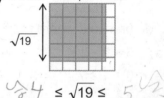

    <u>3</u> ≤ $\sqrt{10}$ ≤ <u>4</u>   <u>2</u> ≤ $\sqrt{7}$ ≤ <u>3</u>   <u>4</u> ≤ $\sqrt{19}$ ≤ <u>5</u>

6. Perfect squares are numbers that have square roots that are whole numbers:
    - Fill in the blanks with the two perfect squares that are closest to the given number.
    - Then find the two whole numbers that the square root lies between.

    a) <u>16</u> ≤ 19 ≤ <u>25</u>   b) <u>9</u> ≤ 13 ≤ <u>16</u>   c) <u>36</u> ≤ 39 ≤ <u>49</u>

    so <u>4</u> ≤ $\sqrt{19}$ ≤ <u>5</u>   so <u>3</u> ≤ $\sqrt{13}$ ≤ <u>4</u>   so <u>6</u> ≤ $\sqrt{39}$ ≤ <u>7</u>

    d) <u>4</u> ≤ 5 ≤ <u>9</u>   e) <u>49</u> ≤ 52 ≤ <u>64</u>   f) <u>16</u> ≤ 17 ≤ <u>25</u>

    so <u>2</u> ≤ $\sqrt{5}$ ≤ <u>3</u>   so <u>7</u> ≤ $\sqrt{52}$ ≤ <u>8</u>   so <u>4</u> ≤ $\sqrt{17}$ ≤ <u>5</u>

7. The area of each shaded strip is 2 cm². What fraction of each 1 cm² square is shaded?

    NOTE: The squares below are not drawn to scale.

    a) 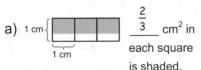 $\frac{2}{3}$ cm² in each square is shaded.

    b) 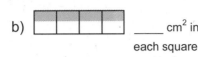 _____ cm² in each square is shaded.

    c) 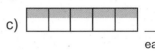 _____ cm² in each square is shaded.

Answer the questions below in your notebook.

8. The length of each side of the shaded square in Figure 1 is $\sqrt{11}$ cm:

    NOTE: The squares below are not drawn to scale.

    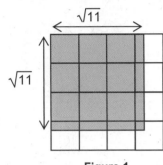

    Figure 1   Figure 2   Figure 3

    a) What is the area of the shaded square in Figure 1?

    b) What is the area of the shaded square in Figure 2?

    c) What is the area of the shaded part in Figure 3?

9. How did you find the area of the shaded part in Figure 3?

10. In Figure 3, seven squares (each of area 1 cm²) are partly shaded. The area of the shaded part is 2 cm². About what fraction of each 1 cm² square in Figure 3 is shaded?

11. Why is your answer in Question 10 an approximation? **HINT: Are all the squares shaded identically?**

12. The area of the shaded region is about $\frac{2}{7}$ cm².

    What is the approximate length of X (in cm)?

    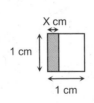

13. a) What is the approximate value of 3 + x (the length of the shaded square)?

    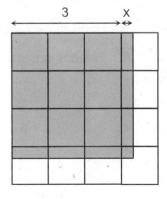

    b) What is the approximate value of $\sqrt{11}$?

14. Use the method above to find the approximate square root of:

    a) $\sqrt{7}$ b) $\sqrt{17}$ c) $\sqrt{29}$

15. Maureen noticed the following pattern:

    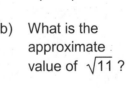

    $\sqrt{11} = 3\frac{2}{7}$ ← difference between 11 and 9 (the largest perfect square less than 11)

    ← difference between 16 and 9 (16 is the next perfect square after 9)

    ← the root of 9

    Use Maureen's pattern to find: a) $\sqrt{28}$ b) $\sqrt{39}$ c) $\sqrt{53}$

1. Label the number line, marking each integer with an 'X' and the correct letter:

   A: $+5$　　　　**B:** -3　　　　**C:** $+7$　　　　**D:** -4　　　　**E:** -6

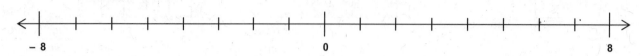

   -8　　　　　　　　　　0　　　　　　　　　　8

2. Write three integers that are less than zero: _____ _____ _____

3. An integer is **less than** another integer if it is **further left** on the number line. Circle the least integer in each pair:

   a) -3 or $+5$　　　b) $+7$ or -2　　　c) $+8$ or $+3$　　　d) -5 or -4　　　e) -7 or -9

4. Write < or > in the box:

   a) $+3$ ☐ $+7$　　b) -5 ☐ $+4$　　c) $+7$ ☐ -2　　d) -4 ☐ -6　　e) -2 ☐ -10

5. Put the integers into the boxes in **increasing** order:

   $+5, -3, +10, -7, -2$ ⟶ ☐ ☐ ☐ ☐ ☐

6. On the number line, mark the number that is:

   A: 2 less than 0　　　**B:** 3 less than 4　　　**C:** 3 greater than -1　　　**D:** 5 greater than -2

   -10　　　　　　　　　　0　　　　　　　　　　10

7. On the number line in Question 6 (above), mark a number that is:

   E: Halfway between $+2$ and $+6$　　　　　　**F:** An equal distance from -8 and -2

   G: The same distance from 0 as -9　　　　　**H:** Twice as far from zero as -4

8. How many units apart are the following integers?

   a) -5 and 2 are _____ units apart.　　　　b) -3 and 3 are _____ units apart.

   c) -8 and -4 are _____ units apart.　　　d) -27 and -17 are _____ units apart.

9.

	Daily Low Temperature	Daily High Temperature
Monday	-8	$+2$
Tuesday	-10	-8
Wednesday	-4	0
Thursday	-17	-5

How much did the temperature change in the course of each day?

Monday _____　　　　Wednesday _____

Tuesday _____　　　　Thursday _____

NS8-64: Adding Integers

 A circle with + 1 inside can represent <u>a gain of 1</u>.
NOTE: Think of a dollar coin that you possess or that is owed to you.

 A circle with − 1 can represent <u>a loss or debt of 1</u>.
NOTE: Think of a dollar coin that you have paid or that you owe to someone else.

Adding + 1 and − 1 gives a result of zero: = 0   (+ 1) + (− 1) = 0

Integers that add to zero are called **opposite integers**.

---

1. Find the net gain or loss by cancelling pairs of opposite integers. Parts a) and e) are already done:

a)

these cancel   *these cancel*   *these cancel*

= − 2

b)

=

c) (+ 1) (+ 1) (+ 1) (− 1) (− 1) (+ 1) (− 1)

=

d) (− 1) (+ 1) (+ 1) (− 1) (+ 1) (− 1) (+ 1)

=

e) (− 1) + (+ 1) + (− 1) + (− 1) + (− 1) + (+ 1)

these cancel   *these cancel*

= − 2

f) (− 1) + (− 1) + (− 1) + (+ 1) + (− 1) + (+ 1)

=

g) (+ 1) + (− 1) + (− 1) + (+ 1) + (+ 1)

=

h) (+ 1) + (+ 1) + (− 1) + (− 1) + (+ 1) + (− 1)

=

2. Draw a model for each sum. Then find the sum by cancelling pairs of opposite integers:

a) (+ 4) + (− 2) = ___ + 2 ___

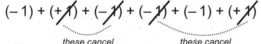

b) (− 2) + (− 1) = ___ − 3 ___

c) (+ 3) + (− 4) = _____

d) (+ 4) + (− 2) = _____

e) (+ 2) + (+ 3) = _____

f) (− 2) + (− 3) = _____

g) (− 3) + (− 2) = _____

h) (− 3) + (+ 3) = _____

Number Sense 2

NS8-65: More Integers

1. Add the numbers by making a model or forming a mental picture of each number:
   HINT: Imagine each integer as a certain number of + 1 and – 1 coins. Before you add, decide: is there a net <u>loss</u> or a net <u>gain</u>?

   a) $(+5) + (-6)$

   =

   b) $(+2) + (-8)$

   =

   c) $(-3) + (+5)$

   =

   d) $(-2) + (-4)$

   =

   e) $(-7) + (+10)$

   =

   f) $(-4) + (+4)$

   =

   g) $(-3) + (-7)$

   =

   h) $(-2) + (-6)$

   =

   i) $(-4) + (-8)$

   =

   j) $(-5) + (+3)$

   =

   k) $(-4) + (-5)$

   =

   l) $(-17) + (+20)$

   =

2. Find the missing numbers:

   a) $(+7) +$ _____ $= +5$

   b) $(-3) +$ _____ $= +1$

   c) $-4 +$ _____ $= -6$

   d) _____ $+ (+2) = -4$

   e) _____ $+ (-5) = +5$

   f) _____ $+ (-8) = -6$

   g) $(-3) +$ _____ $= -7$

   h) _____ $+ (+6) = +8$

   i) $(-2) +$ _____ $= -5$

3. Solve the puzzle by placing the same integer in each shape:

   a) ☐ + ☐ + ☐ $= -6$

   b) ◯ + ◯ + ◯ $= -30$

4.

   If you were to spin the spinner twice and add the two results…

   a) What is the highest total you could score? _____

   b) What is the lowest total you could score? _____

   c) How could you score zero? _____

5. Continue the pattern:

   a) $+10, +5, 0, -5,$ _____, _____, _____, _____, _____

   b) $+10, +8, +6, +4,$ _____, _____, _____, _____, _____

Integers may be represented by arrows (or vectors) on a number line:

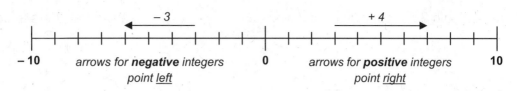

arrows for **negative** integers point <u>left</u>

arrows for **positive** integers point <u>right</u>

To **add** two integers, for example **(+ 4) + (− 6)**, follow these steps…

Step 1:

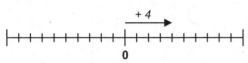

Starting at zero, draw an arrow representing the first integer (in this case, + 4).

Step 2:

So we see that (+ 4) + (− 6) = − 2

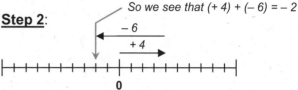

Then, starting at the tip of the first arrow you drew, draw an arrow representing the second integer (−6).

---

1. What integer does each arrow represent? Write the integer on top of the arrow:

a)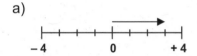

b)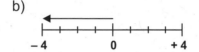

c)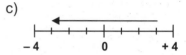

2. Write integers on the arrows. Then fill in the missing integer in each addition statement:

a) (+ 3) + _____ = − 2

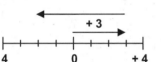

b) (− 2) + _____ = − 4

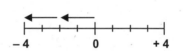

c) (− 4) + _____ = 2

3. Write integers on the arrows and write an addition statement for each picture. Then find the sum:

a)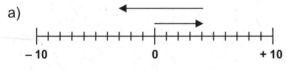

_____

b)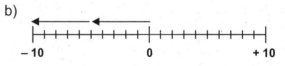

_____

c)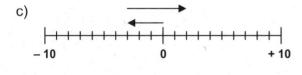

_____

d)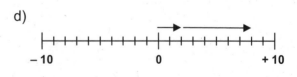

_____

Answer the following questions in your notebook.

4. Draw arrows on a number line to represent the following sums:

a) (− 3) + (− 5)   b) (+ 8) + (− 2)   c) (− 3) + (− 7)   d) (− 6) + (− 2)

5. Use a number line to continue the pattern:

a) + 11, + 8, + 5, + 2, ____, ____, ____   b) − 10, − 8, − 6, − 4, ____, ____, ____

Number Sense 2

Rita was paid $5 to paint a picnic table:

She offered a friend $3 to help:

Rita has a
net gain of $2:

$+5 - 3 = +2$

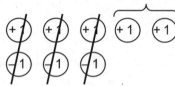

Rita's friend offers to do the work for free:

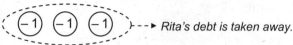 - - ▸ *Rita's debt is taken away.*

Rita now has a net gain of $5:

$+2 - (-3) = +2 + 3 = +5$

Taking away a debt of 3… *… gives a gain of 3*

---

1. Rewrite each difference to show the effect of <u>taking away a **debt**</u>, as in a):

   a)

   $+2 - (-2)$

   $=$ __+2 + 2__

   $=$ __+4__

   b) (+1) (−1) *taken away*
   (+1)
   (+1)

   $+2 - (-1)$

   $=$ _____

   $=$ _____

   c) (+1) (−1)
   (+1) (−1)
   (−1)
   (−1) *taken away*

   $-2 - (-4)$

   $=$ _____

   $=$ _____

   d) (+1) (−1)
   (−1)
   (−1) *taken away*

   $-2 - (-3)$

   $=$ _____

   $=$ _____

2. Rewrite each difference to show the effect of <u>taking away a **gain**</u>, as in a):

   a) (+1) (−1)
   (+1) (−1)
   taken away (−1)
   (−1)

   $-2 - (+2)$

   $=$ __−2 − 2__

   $=$ __−4__

   b) (+1) (−1)
   taken away (−1)
   (−1)
   (−1)

   $-3 - (+1)$

   $=$ _____

   $=$ _____

   c) (+1) (−1)
   (+1) (−1)
   (+1)
   (+1) *taken away*

   $+2 - (+4)$

   $=$ _____

   $=$ _____

   d) (+1) (−1)
   (+1) (−1)
   taken away

   $0 - (+2)$

   $=$ _____

   $=$ _____

3. Complete each computation:

   a) $+5 - (-3)$
   $= +5 + 3$
   $=$

   b) $+4 - (-2)$
   $=$
   $=$

   c) $+3 - (-4)$
   $=$
   $=$

   d) $+6 - (+2)$
   $=$
   $=$

   e) $+7 - (+9)$
   $=$
   $=$

E

Number Sense 2

To represent the difference between the integers + 8 and + 5, you can draw an arrow that starts at + 5 (the number you are subtracting) and ends at + 8. The arrow shows the difference between the numbers:

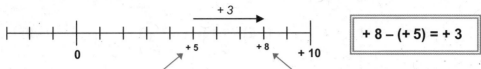

$$+ 8 - (+ 5) = + 3$$

Start at + 5, the number you are subtracting.   *End* at the number you are subtracting from: + 8.

You can find the difference between *any* pair of integers using this method:

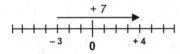 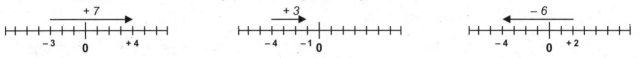

$$\underbrace{(+ 4)}_{end} - \underbrace{(- 3)}_{start} = + 7 \qquad \underbrace{(- 1)}_{end} - \underbrace{(- 4)}_{start} = + 3 \qquad \underbrace{(- 4)}_{end} - \underbrace{(+ 2)}_{start} = - 6$$

---

1. Label the arrow and the points at which the arrow starts and ends. Then write a subtraction statement:

a)   b)   c)

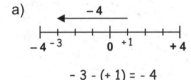 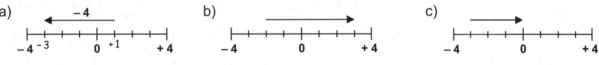 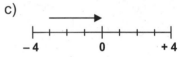

   $- 3 - (+ 1) = - 4$ _____   _____

2. Draw an arrow to represent each difference. Then find the difference:

The arrow should start here

a) + 5 − (− 3) = _____   b) + 6 − (+ 2) = _____   c) + 3 − (+ 2) = _____

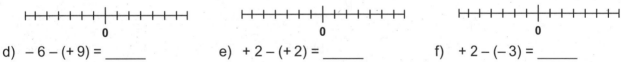  

d) − 6 − (+ 9) = _____   e) + 2 − (+ 2) = _____   f) + 2 − (− 3) = _____

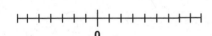 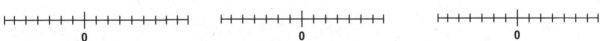 

Answer the remaining questions in your notebook.

3.
Winnipeg Temperatures:	
Monday	+ 2°C
Tuesday	− 10°C
Wednesday	− 17°C

Write a subtraction statement to show how far the temperature fell between:

a) Monday and Tuesday   b) Tuesday and Wednesday

c) Monday and Wednesday

4. An average score in golf is called par. Lei's gulf score was 5 shots above par. Guled's score was 4 shots below par.

   a) Draw an arrow on a number line to represent the distance between their scores.

   b) Write a subtraction statement to represent the distance between their scores.

By convention, the sum $(+2) + (+3)$ may be written as $+2+3$. Similarly, $(+2) + (-3)$ is written $+2-3$ and $(-2) + (-3)$ is written $-2-3$:

$$(+2) + (+3) = +2+3 \qquad (+2) + (-3) = +2-3 \qquad (-2) + (-3) = -2-3$$

A number that doesn't have a sign in front of it is a positive $(+)$ number: $7-8 = +7-8$

----

1. Rewrite each statement in a simpler form:

   a) $+3 + (+5)$ 　　 b) $+7 + (-2)$ 　　 c) $-3 + (-2)$ 　　 d) $-5 + (+3)$ 　　 e) $6 + (-3)$

   　= _____ 　　 = _____ 　　 = _____ 　　 = _____ 　　 = _____

2. Think of a positive integer as money you have gained and a negative number as money you have lost (or paid out).

   Circle the pairs of integers that represent a net loss:

   a) $+8-9$ 　　 b) $+7+2$ 　　 c) $+3-7$ 　　 d) $+2-3$ 　　 e) $-3+8$

   f) $+9+10$ 　　 g) $-2-1$ 　　 h) $+3-4$ 　　 i) $+58-63$ 　　 j) $-20-50$

3. Add the integers:

   HINT: **Start by writing a + or a – sign to show whether you have a net gain or a net loss.**

REMEMBER
Two losses add to a bigger loss: $-7-2 = -9$
A gain and a loss cancel each other: $-8+6 = -2$

   a) $+5-3$ 　　 b) $+2-7$

   　= _____ 　　 = _____

   c) $-4+6$ 　　 d) $+3-9$ 　　 e) $-2-8$ 　　 f) $-17+21$ 　　 g) $3-7$

   　= _____ 　　 = _____ 　　 = _____ 　　 = _____ 　　 = _____

   h) $5-15$ 　　 i) $8-39$ 　　 j) $9+25$ 　　 k) $-6-13$ 　　 l) $-10+24$

   　= _____ 　　 = _____ 　　 = _____ 　　 = _____ 　　 = _____

   m) $0-37$ 　　 n) $62+68$ 　　 o) $8+39$ 　　 p) $52+37$ 　　 q) $83-17$

   　= _____ 　　 = _____ 　　 = _____ 　　 = _____ 　　 = _____

4. Circle all of the negative integers in each question.

   Then combine the positive integers and the negative integers and then find the answer:

Example: $-6 + 4 + 3 - 4$
$= +7 - 10$
$= -3$

   a) $-3+2-5+3$ 　　 b) $-4+5+4-2$ 　　 c) $3-3+5-2+4$ 　　 d) $12-14+7-26$

   　= 　　　 = 　　　 = 　　　 =

   　= 　　　 = 　　　 = 　　　 =

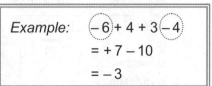

Recall that **sums of integers** can be written in simpler forms:

$$+ 5 + (+ 3) = + 5 + 3 \qquad + 2 + (-5) = + 2 - 5 \qquad - 3 + (-2) = - 3 - 2$$

Differences of integers may also be written in simpler form:

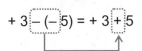 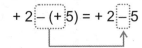

REMEMBER:	+ (+	⇨	+
	+ (−	⇨	−
	− (+	⇨	−
	− (−	⇨	+

Taking away a loss gives a gain.   *Taking away a gain gives a loss.*

- -

1. Simplify each expression and then add to find the result:

   a) $+ 3 + (+ 2)$

   =

   =

   b) $- 5 + (-3)$

   =

   =

   c) $+ 2 - (+ 3)$

   =

   =

   d) $- 4 - (-6)$

   =

   =

   e) $- 11 - (-6)$

   =

   =

   f) $+ 14 + (-8)$

   =

   =

   g) $- 3 + (+ 7)$

   =

   =

   h) $- 25 - (-5)$

   =

   =

   i) $- 2 + (-3) + (+ 4)$

   =

   =

   j) $+ 3 + (-5) + 4$

   =

   =

   k) $- 9 - (+ 8) - (- 12)$

   =

   =

   l) $- 4 + 5 - (- 6) + (- 3)$

   =

   =

2. Fill in the missing integer that will make the statement true:

   a) $(- 3) + \underline{\quad} = - 1$ b) $+ 7 - \underline{\quad} = + 10$ c) $\underline{\quad} - (-4) = - 3$ d) $(-6) + \underline{\quad} = - 10$

3. The integers in each row, column and two diagonals (those including the centre box) in the magic square add up to + 3.

   Find the missing integers:

   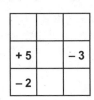

4. The chart shows the average temperatures in winter and summer for three Canadian cities.

   Find the range of temperatures for each city:

City	Avg Winter Temp (°C)	Avg Summer Temp (°C)	Range
Toronto	− 5	20	
Montreal	− 10	21	
Vancouver	− 3	23	

5. Which statements are true and which are false? If you circled false, give a counter example:

   a) The sum of two negative integers is negative.   **T**   **F**

   _____

   b) If you add a negative integer to a positive integer, the result is negative.   **T**   **F**

   _____

Several hundred years ago, mathematicians introduced the idea of **multiplying** and **dividing negative numbers**. They found these operations useful, especially for solving equations.

---

1. Recall that multiplication is a short form for repeated addition:

   Example: 4 × 5 = 5 + 5 + 5 + 5 = 20

   When you multiply a negative integer by a positive integer, you can think of repeated addition:

   Example: 4 × (− 5) = (− 5) + (− 5) + (− 5) + (− 5) = − 20

   Write each product as repeated addition. Then find the answer:

   a) 3 × (−5) =   b) 2 × (−7) =

   c) 4 × (−3) =   d) 4 × (−2) =

2. Represent each product on a number line using arrows to represent the negative integer:
   HINT: Start at 0 each time.

   a) 4 × −3 = ___−12___   b) 5 × (−2) = _____

   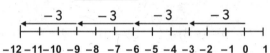

   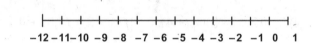

3. If you have a debt of $5 and you triple your debt, you will have a debt of $15: so 3 × −5 = −15. When you multiply a negative number by a positive number, think of increasing the size of debt. Find each product mentally:

   a) 5 × (−6) =   b) 3 × (−6) =   c) 4 × (−3) =

   d) 7 × (−4) =   e) 8 × (−9) =   f) 10 × (−2) =

4. The operation of multiplication **commutes**. When you multiply a pair of positive numbers, you get the same answer no matter what order you multiply the numbers in:

   4 × 7 = 7 × 4   3 × 8 = 8 × 3   a × b = b × a

   Mathematicians <u>defined</u> negative multiplication so that it would also commute.

   Find the product by first changing the order of the numbers:

   a) (− 3) × 2 = ___2 × (− 3) = - 6___   b) (−4) × 7 = _____

5. Multiply mentally:

   a) − 3 × 9 =   b) − 2 × 2 =   c) 7 × (−8) =   d) 4 × (−6) =

   e) − 6 × 7 =   f) − 9 × 4 =   g) − 4 × 6 =   h) 9 × (−9) =

6. In your notebook, write a rule for multiplying a positive number by a negative number.

(continued)

7. Positive numbers satisfy the **distributive law**:

$a \times (b + c) = a \times b + a \times c$ *Example:* $2 \times (3 + 4) = 2 \times 7 = 14$ **also**, $2 \times 3 + 2 \times 4 = 6 + 8 = 14$

Use the distributive law to rewrite each product:

a) $2 \times (5 + 3)$

   $= 2 \times 5 + 2 \times 3$

b) $3 \times (4 + 2)$

   $=$

c) $4 \times (4 + 2)$

   $=$

8. Mathematicians <u>defined</u> negative multiplication to satisfy the <u>distributive law</u>. To see what the product of two negative numbers should be, use the distributive law:

TEACHER: Present several examples like the one below to show students why a negative number times a negative number is a positive number.

Step 1: Pick any pair of **opposite** integers (ie., integers that add to zero).	3 and -3
Step 2: Write an equation for the sum of the integers.	$3 + (-3) = 0$
Step 3: Multiply both sides of your equation by <u>any</u> negative integer (for instance, –2). The right hand side of the equation is still 0 since $-2 \times 0 = 0$.	$-2 \times (3 + (-3)) = -2 \times 0 = 0$
Step 4: Use the distributive law to rewrite the left hand side of the equation.	$-2 \times 3 + (-2) \times (-3) = 0$ $-6 + \underbrace{(-2) \times (-3)} = 0$ *To satisfy the distributive law, this product must be equal to +6, (otherwise the two products do not add to zero).*

The product of two negative integers is a positive integer: $(-2) \times (-3) = +6$

Find the products:

a) $(-3) \times (-5) =$ b) $(-4) \times (-9) =$ c) $(-8) \times (-3) =$ d) $(-2) \times (-5) =$

e) $(-4) \times (-8) =$ f) $(-7) \times (-9) =$ g) $(-8) \times (-6) =$ h) $(-5) \times (-11) =$

9. Rewrite each multiplication statement to find two equivalent division statements. The first two are done for you:

a) $4 \times 3 = 12$

   $12 \div 3 = 4$

   $12 \div 4 = 3$

b) $-4 \times 3 = -12$

   $(-12) \div 3 = -4$

   $(-12) \div (-4) = 3$

c) $(-4) \times (-3) = 12$

   _____

   _____

d) $4 \times (-3) = -12$

   _____

   _____

10. In your notebook, write a rule for the sign of the quotient when you…

a) divide a negative number by a positive number.

b) divide a positive number by a negative number.

c) divide a negative number by a negative number.

11. Find the following quotients:

a) $(-20) \div 4$ b) $(-54) \div (-6)$ c) $(-72) \div (-9)$ d) $80 \div (-10)$ e) $(-16) \div 4$

1. BEDMAS is a way to remember in what order to perform operations in a mathematical expression.

   (1) First perform all questions inside B _____.

   (2) Then calculate E _____.

   (3) Then D _____ and M _____ in order from left to right.

   (4) Then A _____ and S _____ in order from left to right.

Answer the questions below in your notebook.

2. Perform the following calculations using the correct order of operations:

   a) $4 \times (-2) \times 3$

   b) $4 \div (-2) \times 3$

   c) $4 \times (-2) \times (-3)$

   d) $5 \times (-3) + 9$

   e) $5 + (-3) \times 9$

   f) $(-5) \times (-3) + 9$

   g) $5 \times (-3 + 9)$

   h) $1 \times 7 - (-6) \div 2$

   i) $5 - 3 \times (-7) + 4$

   j) $(-8) \div (3 - 7)$

   k) $7 - (3 - 5)$

   l) $(4 - 12) \div (-2)$

   m) $(12 - 3) \times (-4) \div 3$

   n) $(-2) \times (-3) - (4 + 7)$

   o) $(5 - 3) \times (7 - 10)$

   p) $(24 + 2 \times (-6)) \div 4$

   q) $(-3)^2 + 4 \times (-5)$

   r) $3^2 - 5^2$

   s) $(3 - 5)^2$

   t) $(-1)^{20}$

   u) $(-1)^5 - 3$

3. Add brackets where necessary to the following equations to make them true:

   a) $3 - 5 \times 2 = -7$

   b) $3 - 5 \times 2 = -4$

   c) $5 + (-2) \times (-3) = -9$

   d) $5 + (-2) \times (-3) = 11$

   e) $2 - 5 \times 3 + 4 = -5$

   f) $2 - 5 \times 3 + 4 = -9$

   g) $2 - 5 \times 3 + 4 = -21$

   h) $2 - 5 \times 3 + 4 = -33$

   i) $3 - 5^2 = 4$

   j) $2^3 \div 4 - 8 = -2$

   k) $(-2)^3 + 2 \times 4 = 0$

   l) $(-2)^3 + 2 \times 4 = -24$

4. Fill in the missing operation signs to make the statements true.

   a) $(-12) \boxed{} 4 \boxed{} (-2) = -50$

   b) $(-12) \boxed{} 4 \boxed{} (-2) = 6$

   c) $(-12) \boxed{} 4 \boxed{} (-2) = -10$

   d) $(-12) \boxed{} 4 \boxed{} (-2) = -20$

5. Translate the expression into equations and evaluate the expressions:

   Example: Add 7 and 5.   Then divide by 3.   Then add 2.   Answer: $(7 + 5) \div 3 + 2$
   $$= 12 \div 3 + 2$$
   $$= 4 + 2 = 6$$

   a) Multiply -2 and -3
      Subtract 7
      Add 4

   b) Subtract 9 from -6
      Then add 3
      Then divide by -4

   c) Divide 6 by -3
      Then add -10
      Then subtract -12

   d) Add 2 and -8
      Divide by 3
      Subtract 5

6. Write the following expressions in words:

   Example: $7 - 2 \times 3$ Answer: Multiply 2 and 3. Subtract from 7.

   a) $(6 + (-8)) \times 3$

   b) $(7 + (-7)) \div 14$

   c) $4 \times (3 + (-2) \times (-5))$

   d) $(5 - 3) \times 3 (-2)$

7. Evaluate:

   a) $(-2)^{(4 + 2) \div 2}$

   b) $(-2)^{4 + 2 \div 2}$

8. Add brackets to make the equation true:

   $(-2)^{6 \div 3 - 1} = -8$

Earth	+ 20°C
Venus	+ 470°C
Saturn	− 180°C
Mercury	+ 120°C
Jupiter	− 150°C

1. The chart shows the average temperature on 5 planets:
   a) Write the temperatures in order from least to greatest.
   b) What is the difference between the highest and the lowest average temperature?
   c) Which planet has an average temperature 200°C lower than Earth?
   d) Which planet has an average temperature about 6 times greater than Earth?

2. The temperature is 0°C. Answer the questions below using a multiplication statement.

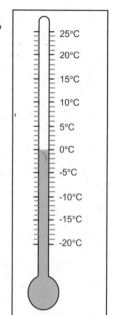

   a) The temperature rises 6°C each hour. What will the temperature be in 3 hours?
      Answer: $(+ 6) \times (+ 3) = + 18$, so the temperature will be + 18°C in 3 hours.

      What will the temperature be in 5 hours? In $2\frac{1}{2}$ hours? In $1\frac{1}{3}$ hours?

      What was the temperature 3 hours ago? $2\frac{1}{2}$ hours ago? $1\frac{1}{3}$ hours ago?

   b) The temperature drops 6°C each hour.
      What will the temperature be in 3 hours? In $2\frac{1}{2}$ hours? In $1\frac{1}{3}$ hours?

      What was the temperature 3 hours ago? $2\frac{1}{2}$ hours ago? $1\frac{1}{3}$ hours ago?

3. Find pairs of integers whose:

   a) sum is − 1 and product is − 20   b) sum is +15 and product is − 100
   c) sum is + 4 and product is − 5   d) sum is − 7 and product is + 12
   e) sum is − 7 and product is + 10   f) sum is − 7 and product is − 144

4. Tasfia estimates that the temperature in Ottawa is half-way between the temperatures in Yellowknife, Northwest Territories and in Tampa, Florida.
   Use Tasfia's estimate to find the missing temperatures:

Day	Temperature in Yellowknife	Temperature in Tampa	Temperature in Ottawa
One	− 15°C	25°C	____°C
Two	____°C	25°C	10°C
Three	− 2°C	____°C	12°C

5. Decide whether each statement is true or false. If the statement is false, change the statement to make it true:
   a) The sum of two opposite integers is always positive.
   b) +5 is opposite to − 3 because they have different signs.
   c) A positive integer is always greater than a negative integer.
   d) The product of two integers will be positive exactly when they have the same sign.

6. What is the result when you divide any nonzero integer by its opposite? *Example:* $3 \div (− 3)$ or $(− 3) \div 3$

7. When a plane takes off, the temperature on the ground is 20°C. The temperature outside the plane decreases by 5°C every time it climbs 1000 m. If the plane is 5000 m above the ground, what is the temperature outside the plane now? What will the temperature outside the plane be when it is 5400 m above the ground?

1. Recall that multiplication is a short form for addition:

    $3 \times 4 = 4 + 4 + 4$ $5 \times 7 = 7 + 7 + 7 + 7 + 7$ $2 \times 9 = 9 + 9$

    Write each product as sum, as in a):

    a) $3 \times \frac{1}{4} = \frac{1}{4} + \frac{1}{4} + \frac{1}{4}$ b) $2 \times \frac{3}{7} =$ c) $4 \times \frac{5}{11} =$

2. Write each sum as a product:

    a) $\frac{1}{2} + \frac{1}{2} + \frac{1}{2} =$ b) $\frac{5}{9} + \frac{5}{9} =$ c) $\frac{3}{4} + \frac{3}{4} + \frac{3}{4} + \frac{3}{4} + \frac{3}{4} =$

Indira multiplies $3 \times \frac{3}{4}$ by making a model with grids and counters,

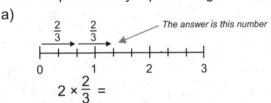

$3 \times \frac{3}{4} \rightarrow$

She makes 3 models of $\frac{3}{4}$.   She rearrange the counters to show the answer. $3 \times \frac{3}{4} = \frac{9}{4} = 2\frac{1}{4}$

---

3. Find the products using Indira's method:

    answers

    a) $2 \times \frac{3}{5} =$

    b) $4 \times \frac{2}{3} =$

    c) $3 \times \frac{5}{6} =$

4. Find the products by representing the multiplication on a number line as in a):
    a)

    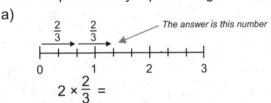

    The answer is this number

    $2 \times \frac{2}{3} =$

    b)

    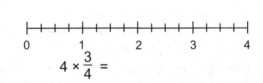

    $4 \times \frac{3}{4} =$

5. Find the products by first writing each product as a sum:

    a) $2 \times \frac{3}{5} =$ b) $3 \times \frac{3}{4} =$ c) $2 \times \frac{4}{7} =$

    d) $5 \times \frac{4}{11} =$ e) $6 \times \frac{3}{7} =$

6. Look at your answers in Question 5. Note that …

    i)   *the numerator of the answer is equal to the whole number times the numerator of the original fraction and…*
    ii) *the denominator of the answer is equal to the denominator of the original fraction.*

    Use this rule to find the products below. Simplify your answer. (Show your work in your notebook.)

    a) $3 \times \frac{4}{6} = \frac{12}{6} = 2$ b) $8 \times \frac{3}{4} =$ c) $5 \times \frac{4}{10} =$ d) $3 \times \frac{6}{9} =$ e) $12 \times \frac{2}{8} =$

Here is $\frac{1}{3}$ of a rectangle | *Here is $\frac{1}{4}$ of $\frac{1}{3}$ of the rectangle* | *How much is $\frac{1}{4}$ of $\frac{1}{3}$?* | *Extend the lines to find out:* $\frac{1}{4}$ of $\frac{1}{3} = \frac{1}{12}$

1. Extend the horizontal line in each picture to find the answer; then write a fraction statement of each figure using the word "of":

    a)   b)   c)   d)   e)

    $\frac{1}{2}$ of $\frac{1}{4} = \frac{1}{8}$

2. Notice that the amounts in Question 1 can be found by multiplying the numerators and denominators of the fractions:

    $\frac{1}{2}$ of $\frac{1}{4} = \frac{1 \times 1}{2 \times 4} = \frac{1}{8}$ $\frac{1}{5}$ of $\frac{1}{3} = \frac{1 \times 1}{5 \times 3}$ $\frac{1}{6}$ of $\frac{1}{2} = \frac{1 \times 1}{6 \times 2}$ (Can you explain why this works?)

    Find the following amounts by multiplying:

    a) $\frac{1}{2}$ of $\frac{1}{5} =$ b) $\frac{1}{2}$ of $\frac{1}{7} =$ c) $\frac{1}{3}$ of $\frac{1}{6} =$ d) $\frac{1}{5}$ of $\frac{1}{7} =$

     Here is $\frac{2}{3}$ of a rectangle | *Here is $\frac{4}{5}$ of $\frac{2}{3}$* | *How much is $\frac{4}{5}$ of $\frac{2}{3}$?* | *Extend the lines to find out:* $\frac{4}{5}$ of $\frac{2}{3} = \frac{8}{15}$ | *Notice:* $\frac{4}{5}$ of $\frac{2}{3} = \frac{4 \times 2}{5 \times 3} = \frac{8}{15}$

3. Write a fraction statement for each figure:

    a)   b)   c)

    $\frac{2}{7}$ of $\frac{3}{4} =$

4. Find the following amounts by multiplying the numerator and denominator of the fractions:

    a) $\frac{2}{3}$ of $\frac{4}{7} =$

    b) $\frac{1}{2}$ of $\frac{3}{5} =$

    c) $\frac{3}{4}$ of $\frac{5}{7} =$

The word "of" in mathematics can be interpreted to mean multiplication. For instance, 2 groups of 6 can be written 2 × 6. Similarly $\frac{1}{2}$ group of 6 (or $\frac{1}{2}$ of 6) can be written $\frac{1}{2}$ × 6. $\frac{2}{3}$ of 6 is 4. But notice also: $\frac{2}{3} \times 6 = \frac{2}{3} + \frac{2}{3} + \frac{2}{3} + \frac{2}{3} + \frac{2}{3} + \frac{2}{3} = \frac{12}{3} = 4$.

5. Multiply the following fractions in your notebook. (Reduce your answers to lowest terms.)

    a) $\frac{2}{3} \times \frac{3}{5}$ b) $\frac{3}{4} \times \frac{5}{7}$ c) $\frac{1}{3} \times \frac{4}{5}$ d) $\frac{4}{6} \times \frac{8}{7}$ e) $\frac{3}{7} \times \frac{8}{9}$

NS8-76: Multiplying Decimals by Decimals

1. Write a fraction statement for each figure:

a)   b)   c)   d)

$\frac{7}{10}$ of $\frac{2}{10}$ = $\frac{14}{100}$

2. Write a fraction statement for each figure. Then write a multiplication statement. Then write an equivalent statement in decimal notation, as in a):

a)   b)   c)   d)

$\frac{7}{10}$ of $\frac{3}{10}$ = $\frac{21}{100}$ _____   _____   _____

$\frac{7}{10}$ × $\frac{3}{10}$ = $\frac{21}{100}$ _____   _____   _____

$.7 × .3 = .21$ _____   _____   _____

3. Find each product by first changing each decimal to a fraction and using the rule for multiplying fractions. Then change your answers back into a decimal:

a) $.3 × .7 = \frac{3}{10} × \frac{7}{10} = \frac{21}{100} = .21$ b) $.5 × .4 =$

c) $.2 × .8 =$ d) $.3 × .6 =$

e) $.5 × .9 =$ f) $.4 × .3 =$

g) $.23 × .5 =$ h) $.05 × .4 =$

Look at your answers in Question 3. Notice that the number of decimal places in each answer is always the same as the total number of decimal places in the two numbers being multiplied. This suggests a fast way of multiplying decimals:

Example: $.28 × .4$	**Step 1**	**Step 2**
	Multiply the decimals as if they were whole numbers:	.28 has two decimal places, .4 has one decimal place. So the product should have 2 + 1 = 3 decimals places:
	$28 × 4 = 112$	$.28 × .4 = .112$

4. Using the rule given above, multiply the following decimals in your notebook:

a) $.5 × .8$ b) $.7 × .9$ c) $.2 × .6$ d) $.15 × .8$ e) $.26 × .3$

f) $.4 × .67$ g) $.32 × .9$ h) $.04 × .7$ i) $.2 × .7$ j) $.8 × .46$

1.

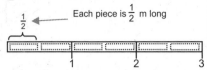

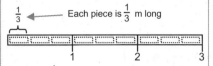

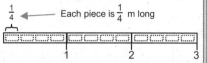

| James divides a 3 m ribbon into $\frac{1}{2}$ m sized pieces. | Kelly divides the same ribbon into $\frac{1}{3}$ m sized pieces. | Kirk divides the same ribbon into $\frac{1}{4}$ m sized pieces. |

Two $\frac{1}{2}$ metre pieces fit into each metre, so... $3 \div \frac{1}{2} = 3 \times 2$

Three $\frac{1}{3}$ metre pieces fit into each metre, so... $3 \div \frac{1}{3} = 3 \times 3$

Four $\frac{1}{4}$ metre pieces fit into each metre, so... $3 \div \frac{1}{4} = 3 \times 4$

Find the following quotients by using a model:

a) $4 \div \frac{1}{3} = \underline{4} \times \underline{3} = \underline{12}$ b) $5 \div \frac{1}{2} = \underline{} \times \underline{} = \underline{}$ c) $5 \div \frac{1}{3} = \underline{} \times \underline{} = \underline{}$

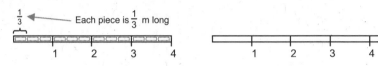

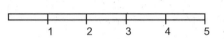

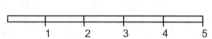

2. In general, $a \div \frac{1}{b} = a \times b$. In your notebook, use this rule to find each quotient:

a) $10 \div \frac{1}{3}$ b) $9 \div \frac{1}{5}$ c) $8 \div \frac{1}{4}$ d) $7 \div \frac{1}{7}$ e) $8 \div \frac{1}{6}$ f) $6 \div \frac{1}{6}$

3. Gerome wants to divide a 4 m ribbon into $\frac{2}{5}$ sized pieces:

Step 1:

He knows that 20 fifth ($\frac{1}{5}$) sized pieces fit into 4 m since $4 \times 5 = 20$:

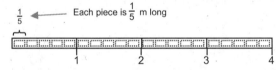

Step 2:

But $\frac{2}{5}$ m is twice as long as $\frac{1}{5}$ m.

So Gerome divides his answer from Step 1 by 2:
$(4 \times 5) \div 2 = 10$ two-fifth sized pieces will fit into 4m.

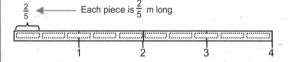

Find the following quotients and complete the model provided, as in a):

a) $4 \div \frac{1}{3} = \underline{4} \times \underline{3} = \underline{12}$

So $4 \div \frac{2}{3} = \underline{12} \div \underline{2} = \underline{6}$

b) $2 \div \frac{1}{5} = \underline{} \times \underline{} = \underline{}$

So $2 \div \frac{2}{5} = \underline{} \div \underline{} = \underline{}$

c) $3 \div \frac{1}{4} = \underline{} \times \underline{} = \underline{}$

So $3 \div \frac{3}{4} = \underline{} \div \underline{} = \underline{}$

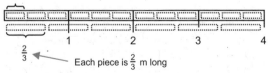

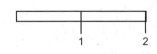

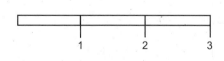

4. Find the quotients:

a) $4 \div \frac{2}{5} = (\underline{4} \times \underline{5}) \div \underline{2}$

$= \underline{10}$

b) $6 \div \frac{2}{5} = (\underline{} \times \underline{}) \div \underline{}$

$= \underline{}$

c) $2 \div \frac{3}{7} = (\underline{} \times \underline{}) \div \underline{}$

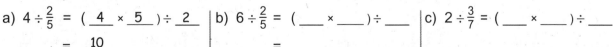

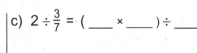

Answer the questions below in your notebook.

1. In general, $a \div \frac{b}{c} = (a \times c) \div b$. But then $a \div \frac{b}{c} = a \times \frac{c}{b}$. Use this rule to find each quotient:

   a) $6 \div \frac{3}{4} = 6 \times \frac{4}{3} = \frac{24}{3} = 8$.
   b) $3 \div \frac{3}{8}$
   c) $8 \div \frac{4}{5}$
   d) $10 \div \frac{2}{5}$
   e) $10 \div \frac{5}{6}$

2. Find each quotient. What do you notice?

   a) $6 \div 2$
   b) $(6 \times 2) \div (2 \times 2)$
   c) $(6 \times 5) \div (2 \times 5)$
   BONUS: d) $(6 \times \frac{1}{3}) \div (2 \times \frac{1}{3})$

   In general, how does $a \div b$ compare to $(a \times c) \div (b \times c)$?

3. Divide the numbers below by first changing the decimals to whole numbers.

   Example: $2.7 \div .2 = (2.7 \times 10) \div (.2 \times 10) = 27 \div 2 = 13.5$

   a) $4.5 \div .5$
   b) $1.8 \div .3$
   c) $2.4 \div .4$
   d) $1.5 \div .3$
   e) $3.8 \div .2$
   f) $4.8 \div .6$
   g) $6.4 \div .8$
   h) $5.4 \div .6$
   i) $2.1 \div .2$
   j) $7.2 \div .8$
   k) $4.6 \div .4$
   l) $8.2 \div .8$
   BONUS:
   m) $0.27 \div 0.03$
   n) $4.92 \div 0.16$

   To find $27 \div 2$
   $$\begin{array}{r} 13.5 \\ 2\overline{)27.0} \\ -2 \\ \hline 07 \\ -6 \\ \hline 10 \\ -10 \\ \hline 0 \end{array}$$

4. Fill in the blanks to make the quotients equal:

   a) $\frac{4}{5} \div \frac{3}{4} = \left[\frac{4}{5} \times \frac{4}{3}\right] \div \left[\frac{3}{4} \times \frac{4}{3}\right]$
   b) $\frac{3}{4} \div \frac{2}{5} = \left[\frac{3}{4} \times \underline{}\right] \div \left[\frac{2}{5} \times \frac{5}{2}\right]$
   c) $\frac{2}{3} \div \frac{1}{2} = \left[\frac{2}{3} \times \underline{}\right] \div \left[\frac{1}{2} \times \frac{2}{1}\right]$

   TEACHER: Give your students a lot of practice with this type of question before moving on.

5. Find each product. Reduce your answers to lowest terms. What do you notice?
   In general, what is $\frac{a}{b} \times \frac{b}{a}$?

   a) $\frac{3}{4} \times \frac{4}{3}$
   b) $\frac{2}{5} \times \frac{5}{2}$
   c) $\frac{3}{7} \times \frac{7}{3}$
   d) $\frac{10}{7} \times \frac{7}{10}$
   e) $\frac{3}{11} \times \frac{11}{3}$

6. Explain why $\frac{3}{4} \div \frac{2}{5} = \frac{3}{4} \times \frac{5}{2}$. **HINT: Use your answers to Questions 4 and 5.**

7. In general, $\frac{a}{b} \div \frac{c}{d} = \frac{a}{b} \times \frac{d}{c}$. Use this rule to find each quotient. Express your answers in lowest terms:

   a) $\frac{3}{5} \div \frac{2}{3} = \frac{3}{5} \times \frac{3}{2} = \frac{9}{10}$
   b) $\frac{3}{5} \div \frac{2}{5}$
   c) $\frac{1}{3} \div \frac{5}{6}$
   d) $\frac{1}{5} \div \frac{3}{8}$
   e) $\frac{3}{7} \div \frac{4}{9}$
   f) $\frac{5}{8} \div \frac{2}{3}$

8. Divide by first changing all mixed fractions to improper fractions:
   Example: $3\frac{1}{2} \div \frac{2}{3} = \frac{7}{2} \div \frac{2}{3} = \frac{7}{2} \times \frac{3}{2} = \frac{21}{4} = 5\frac{1}{4}$

   a) $2\frac{1}{2} \div \frac{1}{2}$
   b) $4\frac{1}{2} \div \frac{1}{4}$
   c) $5\frac{6}{8} \div \frac{1}{4}$
   d) $3\frac{3}{5} \div \frac{1}{10}$
   e) $1\frac{2}{3} \div \frac{1}{12}$

Answer the questions below in your notebook.

1. Evaluate.

   a) $\left[\dfrac{2}{3} + \dfrac{1}{2}\right] \times \dfrac{1}{4}$

   b) $\dfrac{2}{3} + \dfrac{1}{2} \times \dfrac{1}{4}$

   c) $\dfrac{3}{2} + \dfrac{1}{4} \times \dfrac{3}{4}$

   d) $\dfrac{3}{2} \times \left[\dfrac{1}{4} \div \dfrac{3}{4}\right]$

   e) $\dfrac{5}{2} \div \dfrac{3}{4} \times \dfrac{4}{5}$

   f) $\dfrac{5}{2} \div \left[\dfrac{3}{4} \times \dfrac{4}{5}\right]$

   g) $\dfrac{2}{3} + \dfrac{1}{2} - \dfrac{1}{4}$

   h) $\dfrac{2}{3} + \left[\dfrac{1}{2} - \dfrac{1}{4}\right]$

   i) $\dfrac{2}{3} - \dfrac{1}{4} + \dfrac{1}{2}$

   j) $\dfrac{2}{3} - \left[\dfrac{1}{4} + \dfrac{1}{2}\right]$

   k) $\dfrac{2}{3} - \dfrac{1}{4} \times \dfrac{1}{2}$

   l) $\left[\dfrac{2}{3} - \dfrac{1}{4}\right] \times \dfrac{1}{2}$

2. Evaluate.

   a) $(.7 + .3) \div .2$

   b) $.8 + .3 \div .6$

   c) $3.75 - .75 \div .25$

   d) $(3.75 - .75) \div .25$

   e) $.75 \div .2 + .3$

   f) $.75 \div (.2 + .3)$

3. Remove any brackets that are not necessary.
   NOTE: In some expressions, all brackets will be necessary.

   a) $\dfrac{2}{3} + \left[\dfrac{1}{2} - \dfrac{1}{3}\right]$

   b) $\dfrac{2}{3} \times \left[\dfrac{1}{2} - \dfrac{1}{3}\right]$

   c) $\left[\dfrac{1}{2} \times \dfrac{1}{3}\right] + \left[\dfrac{1}{3} - \dfrac{1}{4}\right]$

   d) $\left[\dfrac{1}{2} - \left[\dfrac{1}{3} + \dfrac{1}{4}\right]\right] \times \dfrac{1}{5}$

4. Add brackets to make the following equation true:

   a) $.5 + 1.5 \times .1 = .2$

   b) $.1 + .5 \times .3 + .7 = .88$

   c) $.1 + .5 \times .3 + .7 = .6$

   d) $.1 + .5 \times .3 + .7 = .95$

   e) $\dfrac{1}{3} + \dfrac{2}{3} \times \dfrac{1}{2} - \dfrac{1}{4} = \dfrac{1}{4}$

   f) $\dfrac{1}{3} + \dfrac{2}{3} \times \dfrac{1}{2} - \dfrac{1}{4} = \dfrac{5}{12}$

5. By adding brackets, find at least two different answers:

   Example: $\dfrac{1}{5} + \dfrac{1}{3} \div \dfrac{1}{4} \times \dfrac{1}{2}$ has 5 different answers, including…

   $$\left[\left[\dfrac{1}{5} + \dfrac{1}{3}\right] \div \dfrac{1}{4}\right] \times \dfrac{1}{2} = \dfrac{8}{15} \times 4 \times \dfrac{1}{2} = \dfrac{32}{30} = \dfrac{16}{15} = 1\dfrac{1}{15}$$

   a) $\dfrac{1}{5} + \dfrac{1}{3} \times \dfrac{1}{4} \div \dfrac{1}{2}$

   b) $\dfrac{1}{5} + \dfrac{1}{3} \times \dfrac{1}{4} \div \dfrac{1}{2}$

   c) $\dfrac{1}{5} + \dfrac{1}{3} - \dfrac{1}{4} + \dfrac{1}{2}$

   d) $.5 \times .4 - .3$

   e) $.75 \div .25 \times .5 \div .2$

   f) $.5 \div .3 + .7 - .2$

1. a) $\frac{65}{100}$ is between $\frac{60}{100}$ and $\frac{70}{100}$ or between $\frac{6}{10}$ and $\frac{7}{10}$.

    b) $\frac{37}{100}$ is between $\frac{}{100}$ and $\frac{}{100}$ or between $\frac{}{10}$ and $\frac{}{10}$.

    c) $\frac{44}{100}$ is between $\frac{}{100}$ and $\frac{}{100}$ or between $\frac{}{10}$ and $\frac{}{10}$.

    d) $\frac{5}{100}$ is between $\frac{}{100}$ and $\frac{}{100}$ or between $\frac{}{10}$ and $\frac{}{10}$.

2. Which two decimals is each fraction between?

    a) _0.6_ $< \frac{65}{100} <$ _0.7_   b) ____ $< \frac{37}{100} <$ ____   c) ____ $< \frac{44}{100} <$ ____   d) ____ $< \frac{52}{100} <$ ____

3. Write each fraction as a decimal.

    a) $\frac{47}{100}$ b) $\frac{34}{100}$ c) $\frac{49}{100}$ d) $\frac{9}{100}$ e) $\frac{7}{10}$ f) $\frac{8}{10}$

4. Write each fraction as an equivalent fraction and then as a decimal.

    a) $\frac{1}{2} = \frac{}{10} =$ ____   b) $\frac{3}{25} = \frac{}{100} =$ ____   c) $\frac{7}{20} = \frac{}{100} =$ ____

    d) $\frac{4}{5} = \frac{}{10} =$ ____   e) $\frac{326}{500} = \frac{}{1000} =$ ____   f) $\frac{9}{40} = \frac{}{1000} =$ ____

5. Change each fraction to a decimal by long division.

    a) 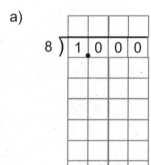 $\frac{1}{8} =$ _____

    b) 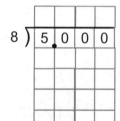 $\frac{5}{8} =$ _____

    c) 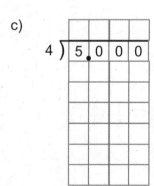 $\frac{5}{4} =$ _____

    d) 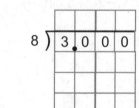 $\frac{3}{8} =$ _____

Number Sense 2

6. Find the decimal value of each fraction to 3 decimal places:

a)
$3 \overline{)\ 1\ 0\ 0\ 0}$ $\frac{1}{3} \approx$ _____

b)
$3 \overline{)\ 2\ 0\ 0\ 0}$ $\frac{2}{3} \approx$ _____

c)
$6 \overline{)\ 1\ 0\ 0\ 0}$ $\frac{1}{6} \approx$ _____

d)
$6 \overline{)\ 5\ 0\ 0\ 0}$ $\frac{5}{6} \approx$ _____

7. Use the pattern you found in Question 6 to predict the decimal value of each fraction to 6 decimal places:

a) $\frac{1}{3} \approx$. _ _ _ _ _ _

b) $\frac{2}{3} \approx$. _ _ _ _ _ _

c) $\frac{5}{6} \approx$. _ _ _ _ _ _

8. To express a repeating decimal like 0.0909090909… we write a line over the repeating part,
    so $0.\overline{09}$ = 0.09090909… and $0.1\overline{90}$ = 0.190909090…

    Find the missing digits in each expression:

a) $0.\overline{3} \approx 0.\ \underline{3}$ _ _ _ _ _ _

b) $0.0\overline{3} \approx 0.\ \underline{0}\ \underline{3}$ _ _ _ _ _

c) $0.\overline{817} \approx 0.\ \underline{8}\ \underline{1}\ \underline{7}$ _ _ _ _ _

d) $0.\overline{54} \approx 0.\ \underline{5}\ \underline{4}$ _ _ _ _ _

e) $0.8\overline{17} \approx 0.\ \underline{8}\ \underline{1}\ \underline{7}$ _ _ _ _

f) $0.7\overline{1} \approx 0.\ \underline{7}\ \underline{1}$ _ _ _ _ _

9. Write each group of numbers in order from least to greatest:

a)   0.4   0.4$\overline{2}$ 0.$\overline{42}$ 0.42

b)   0.16   0.$\overline{1}$ 0.1$\overline{6}$ 0.$\overline{16}$

c)   0.387   0.38$\overline{7}$ 0.3$\overline{87}$ 0.$\overline{387}$

d)   0.546   0.54$\overline{6}$ 0.5$\overline{46}$ 0.$\overline{546}$

e)   0.383   0.38$\overline{3}$ 0.3$\overline{83}$ 0.$\overline{383}$

f)   0.786   0.78$\overline{6}$ 0.7$\overline{86}$ 0.$\overline{786}$

10. Find the decimal representations of the fractions by long division:

a) $\frac{1}{11}$ b) $\frac{2}{11}$ c) $\frac{3}{11}$ d) $\frac{4}{11}$

11. Use the pattern you found in Question 10 to find…

a) $\frac{5}{11}$ b) $\frac{6}{11}$ c) $\frac{7}{11}$ d) $\frac{8}{11}$ e) $\frac{9}{11}$

12. Bilal wants to represent $\frac{1}{11}$ as a decimal using base ten materials. What problem will he run into?

13. Explain why $.6 \leq .\overline{6} \leq .7$.

Answer the following questions in your notebook.

1. I am a 2-digit perfect square.
   When my digits are multiplied together, I am still a perfect square. What number am I?

2. I am a perfect square with square root between 30 and 40.
   My last digit is 5.
   What number am I?

3. I am a 3-digit number between 600 and 700.
   My first two digits form a 2-digit perfect square.
   My last digit is its square root. What number am I?

4. Clarissa wants to pour $2\frac{2}{5}$ L of lemonade into $\frac{2}{3}$ L bottles. How many bottles can he fill?

5. Rennish wants to cut a 4.62 m board into pieces .3 m long. How many pieces can he cut?

6. Find two whole numbers that multiply to 60 and add to…

   a) 61   b) 23   c) 17

   Can you find two whole numbers that multiply to 60 and add to 25?

7. Find three whole numbers (not necessarily different) that …
   a) multiply to 12 and add to 8.
   b) multiply to 20 and add to 9.
   c) multiply to 225 and add to 31.

8. An 8-slice pizza is shared among 3 people. Mayah eats 2 pieces, Tegan eats 3 pieces and Matias eats 3 pieces. The pizza costs $12.99 plus a 14% tax. How much should each person pay?

9. A 24-case of juice costs $5.49 and is shared among 4 people.
   Andranik drinks 7 cans, Ceilidh drinks 11 cans, Huy drinks 4 cans and Sayaka drinks 2 cans.
   After the 14% sales tax is added, how much should each person pay?

10. Two hockey goalies, Dillon and Melissa, are comparing their records.
    Dillon saved 53 out of 60 shots in 3 games. Melissa saved 65 out of 70 shots in 2 games. Find:

    a) The percentage of shots each person saved (to one decimal place) and
    b) The average number of goals allowed per game by each player (to one decimal place).
    c) Who do you think is the better goalie? Why?

11. If you breathe in and out about 21 times a minute, about how many times would you breathe in and out during a year?

12. Two 4-digit numbers are composed of 4 different digits. What is the largest possible difference between them?

13. Calculate $\frac{2}{3}(-1)^{18} + \frac{4}{5}(-1)^{19}$. Check your answer with a calculator.

    HINT: Find $(-1)^2$; $(-1)^3$; $(-1)^4$ ... Do you see a pattern in the answers?

14. You buy a sweater that costs $28.00 plus an 8% sales tax.
    If you wear the sweater 100 times, about how much does it cost you each time you wear it?

15. There is one time zone for each hour of the day.
    The distance around the Earth's equator through 3 time zones is 5 000 km.
    What fraction of the Earth's circumference is this?
    What is the Earth's circumference?

16. Philip gave away 45% of his hockey cards.

    a) What **fraction** of his cards did he **keep**?

    b) Philip put his remaining cards in a scrapbook.

       Each page held 18 cards and he filled $23\frac{5}{6}$ pages.

       How many cards did he put in the book?

    c) How many cards did he have before he gave part of his collection away?

17. 24-karat gold is pure, so that 12-karat gold is 50% pure and 18-karat gold is 75% pure.

    a) What percentage of pure gold is 15-karat gold?

    b) Rita has a gold bracelet weighing 50 g.

       It is 15-karat gold. If pure gold costs $23.64/g,

       what is a fair price for the bracelet?

18. A Fibonacci sequence is a sequence where each number is the sum of the previous two numbers.

    Example: 1, 2, 3, 5, 8, 13, 21 … is a Fibonacci sequence.

    Verify that each sequence below begins a Fibonacci sequence.
    Continue each sequence for 3 more terms:

    a) $\frac{2}{3}$, $\frac{-3}{5}$, $\frac{1}{15}$

    b) $\frac{9}{11}$, $.\overline{54}$, $\frac{3}{11}$

    c) $-.1$, $.1$, 0

ME8-25: Mass

Mass measures the amount of substance in a thing. Grams (g) and kilograms (kg) are units for measuring weight or mass.

One kilogram is equal to 1000 grams.

Things with a mass of about one **gram**:
✓ A paper clip
✓ A dime
✓ A chocolate chip

Things with a mass of about one **kilogram**:
✓ A one litre bottle of water
✓ A bag of 200 nickels
✓ A squirrel

One gram is equal to 1000 milligrams (mg): a milligram is 1000 times smaller than a gram. Milligrams are used to measure the mass of <u>very</u> small objects. A flea has a mass of about 10 mg.

- -

1. Estimate the mass of the following things, in grams:
    REMEMBER: A one litre bottle of water has a mass of 1 kg or 1000 g.

    a) a pen _____   b) an apple _____   c) this workbook _____

2. Can you name an object that has a mass of about one gram? _____

3. The approximate mass of each coin is given below:

Penny	2.5 grams
Nickel	5 grams
Dime	1 gram
Quarter	6 grams
Loonie	7 grams

    a) What would be the mass of 75¢ in nickels? _____

    b) What would be the mass of 15 dimes? _____

    c) What would be the mass of $2.00 in quarters? _____

    d) What would be the mass of 200 loonies? _____

    e) How many quarters would have the same mass as 24 nickels?

    _____

    f) How many pennies would have the same mass as 2 nickels?

    _____

4. Change the following measurements to grams:

    a) 5 kg _____   b) 27 kg _____   c) 350 kg _____   d) 700 kg _____

5. a) Change the mass of a nickel and a quarter (given in Question 3) into milligrams:

    Nickel: _____   Quarter: _____

    b) How many milligrams heavier than a dime is a loonie? _____

6. Here are some primate masses:
    Gorilla 175 kg, Baboon 35 kg, Squirrel monkey 500 kg, Pygmy Mouse Lemur 30 g:

    a) How many grams does a gorilla weigh? _____

    b) How many squirrel monkeys weigh 1 kg? _____

    c) About how many times heavier than a mouse lemur is a baboon? _____

E

Measurement 2

ME8-26: Capacity

The **capacity** of a container is how much it can hold. For example, the capacity of a regular carton of milk is 1 L.

Litres (L) and millilitres (mL) are the basic units for measuring capacity → 1 litre (L) = 1000 millilitres (mL)

Some sample capacities:

1 teaspoon = 5 mL	1 can of pop = 350 mL	1 regular carton of juice = 1 L
1 tube of toothpaste = 75 mL	1 large bottle of shampoo = 750 mL	1 large can of paint = 3 to 5 L

----

1. Would you use millilitres (mL) or litres (L) to measure...

   a) a glass of water?   b)   a bath tub?   c) a swimming pool?   d) a rain drop?

2. Clare fills a measuring cup with 40 mL of water.
   She pours out some water and notices there are 30 mL left. How much water did she pour out?

3. What do you need to multiply a measurement in litres by to change it to millilitres? _____

4. Change the following measurements to millilitres:

   a) 5 L = _____   b) 2 L = _____   c) 12 L = _____   d) 47 L = _____

5. Which will contain more shampoo, four 250 mL bottles or three 300 mL bottles?_____

6. Jenna is carrying groceries. In her bag there is:
   • 1 L of milk,   • a 500 mL bottle of olive oil,   • a 500 mL bottle of vinegar,   • and a 700 mL jar of tomato sauce.

   What is the total capacity of the items in mL?   _____

Answer the remaining questions in your notebook.

7. For each recipe...

   a) Circle the measurements of capacity. Underline the measurements of mass.

   b) Total the measurements of mass for the birthday cake.

   c) Total the measurements of capacity for ice cream.

   Ice Cream
   1 L fresh fruit
   50 mL lemon juice
   250 mL heavy cream
   250 mL light cream
   150 g sugar

   Tomato Sauce
   30 mL olive oil
   800 mL can of tomatoes
   30 mL tomato paste
   5 g fresh oregano
   2 g fresh basil

   Birthday Cake
   115 g butter
   300 g sugar
   2 eggs
   280 g flour
   150 mL milk

8. For each of the following capacities, how many containers would be needed to make a litre? Explain:

   a) 100 mL   b) 200 mL   c) 500 mL   d) 250 mL

9. A recipe for punch that will serve 12 people calls for 75 mL of orange juice.
   How many mL of orange juice would you need to make enough punch for 36 people? Explain.

ME8-27: The Metric System

1. a) How many centimetres are in a metre? _____

    b) How many cents are in a dollar? _____

    c) How many years are in a century? _____

    d) What do you think the Latin word "centum" means? _____

2. a) How many metres are in a kilometre? _____

    b) How many grams are in a kilogram? _____

    c) What do you think the Greek prefix "kilo" means? _____

3. a) How many decimetres are in a metre? _____

    b) How many years are in a decade? _____

    c) How many sides does a decagon have? _____

    d) What do you think the Latin word "deca" means? _____

4. a) How many millimetres are in a metre? _____

    b) How many millilitres are in a litre? _____

    c) How many milligrams are in a gram? _____

    d) What do you think the Latin word "mille" means? _____

5. a) A millimetre is ___1000___ times ___smaller___ than a metre.

    b) A milligram is _____ times _____ than a gram.

    c) A kilometre is _____ times _____ than a metre.

    d) A centimetre is _____ times _____ than a metre.

6. How many times smaller or larger are the first units than the second units? (Write S if the first unit is smaller and L if it is larger)

    a) mL are ___1000 × s___ than L.

    b) mm are _____ than dm.

    c) mm are _____ than m.

    d) g are _____ than mg.

    e) dm are _____ than cm.

    g) m are _____ than cm.

    f) kg are _____ than g.

    h) km are _____ than m.

> **REMEMBER:**
>
> km
> kg
>
> increasing size
>
> m
> g
> L
> dm
> cm
> mm
> mg
> mL
>
> Units <u>increase</u> in size going up the stairway:
> - 1 step = 10 × larger
> - 2 steps = 100 × larger
> - 3 steps = 1000 × larger

jump math
MULTIPLYING POTENTIAL

Measurement 2

7. Change the units by shifting the decimal:
   REMEMBER: if the new unit is larger you need less of the unit, so you shift the decimal left.

   a) ____100____ × ____S____

   6.5.8 m = ____658____ cm

   b) _____ × _____

   8 0 0 0 mL = _____ L

   c) _____ × _____

   3 6 0 0 g = _____ kg

   d) _____ × _____

   1.9 L= _____ mL

   e) _____ × _____

   1 8 m = _____ dm

   f) _____ × _____

   0.5 3 7 g = _____ mg

   g) _____ × _____

   7 1 0 0 0 mg = _____ kg

   h) _____ × _____

   9 6 dm = _____ km

   i) _____ × _____

   4.7 mL = _____ L

8. Compare the measurements by writing > or < in the box. The first one is done for you.
   HINT: Change the larger unit into the smaller unit.

   a) 2.5 m [ ] 175 cm

       250 cm [>] 175 cm

   b) 3 L [ ] 2 752 mL

   c) 2.7 kg [ ] 2 683 g

   d) 5 m [ ] 678 cm

   e) 3.95 dm [ ] 4.2 cm

   f) 275 mg [ ] .3 g

9. Underline the digit corresponding to the unit of measurement given in the box:

   a) [cm] 3.2 7 5 m   b) [mL] 2.8 7 6 L   c) [mm] 8.2 0 3 m   d) [g] 5.3 8 2 kg

   e) [dm] 3 8.2 5 m   f) [L] 3 8 7 5 mL   g) [mg] 3.8 5 2 3 g   h) [kg] 5 4 3 1.1 2 g

Answer the remaining questions in your notebook.

10. Write each mixed measurement as a decimal in the larger unit as shown in the example:

   | *Example*:   9 g 85 mg = 9 g $\frac{85}{1000}$ g = 9.085 g |

   a) 5 g 27 mg   b) 3 km 275 m   c) 9 L 2 mL   d) 27 m 12 mm   e) 807 kg 5 g

11. Cheese costs $9.00 per kg. How much would 150 g of cheese cost?

ME8-28: Changing Units of Area

1. Each of the small squares in Figure 1 has sides 1 cm and area 1 cm² :

   NOTE: Diagram not drawn to scale.

   a) How many 1 cm² squares cover the large square? _____

   b) What is the area of the large square in cm²? _____

   c) How long are the sides of the large square in dm? _____

   d) A dm² is _____ times larger than a cm².

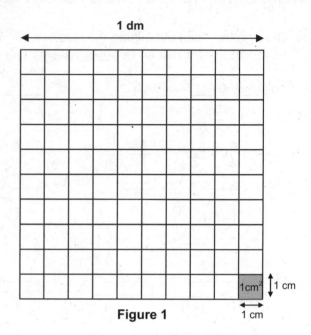

Figure 1

1 dm

1 cm² 1 cm

1 cm

2. a) Change 2700 cm² to dm²

   i) The new units are __100__ times _bigger_

   ii) So I need __100__ times _fewer_ units

   iii) so I ___divide___ by ___100___

   2700 cm² = ___27___ dm²

   b) Change 54 cm² to dm²

   i) The new units are _____ times _____

   ii) So I need _____ times _____ units

   iii) so I _____ by _____

   54 cm² = _____ dm²

   c) Change 72 dm² to cm²

   i) The new units are _____ times _____

   ii) So I need _____ times _____ units

   iii) so I _____ by _____

   72 dm² = _____ cm²

   d) Change .63 dm² to cm²

   i) The new units are _____ times _____

   ii) So I need _____ times _____ units

   iii) so I _____ by _____

   .63 dm² = _____ cm²

3. Change the units by following the steps in question 2 in your head:

   a) 5 dm² = _____ cm²

   b) .9 dm² = _____ cm²

   c) 3 cm² = _____ dm²

   d) 195 cm² = _____ dm²

   e) 1.4 cm² = _____ dm²

   f) 0.05 dm² = _____ cm²

jump math
MULTIPLYING POTENTIAL.

Measurement 2

4. Figure 2 shows a square metre:
   NOTE: Diagram not drawn to scale.

   a) How many dm are in a m? _____

   b) How many dm² would fit into 1 m²? _____

5. Ken says:
   "There are 10 dm along each side of a metre squared.
   So 10 × 10 = 100 dm² will fit into 1 m²
   or 1 m² = 10 × 10 dm² = 100 dm²" (see Figure 2)

   Use Ken's reasoning to fill in the blanks below:
   NOTE: Pictures are not drawn to scale.

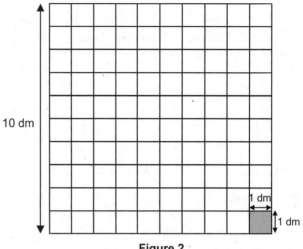

Figure 2

a)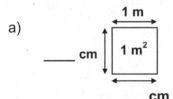

1 m² = _____ × _____ cm²

= _____ cm²

b)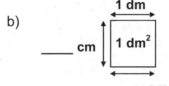

1 dm² = _____ × _____ cm²

= _____ cm²

c)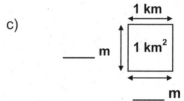

1 km² = _____ × _____ m²

= _____ m²

6. Use your answers above to fill in the statements below:

   a) m² are _____
      times larger than cm²

   b) m² are _____
      times larger than dm²

   c) km² are _____
      times larger than m²

Answer the following questions in your notebook.

7. Change the following units. (questions k) to o) are challenging.)

   a) 7 m² to dm²   b) 7000 dm² to m²   c) 631 cm² to dm²   d) 3 dm² to cm²   e) 9321 dm² to m²

   f) 21 cm² to m²   g) 980 cm² to dm²   h) 5.4 dm² to cm²   i) 4700 cm² to m²   j) .007 m² to cm²

   k) 4 km² to m²   l) 96421 m² to km²   m) 2.7 dm² to mm²   n) 6.93 m² to mm²   o) .08 m² to mm²

8. Erik says a rectangle with a length of 4 m and a height of 50 cm has an area of 200 cm².
   What mistake did he make? Explain.

9. A rectangle has width 4 cm and a perimeter 0.18 m. What is the area?

10. Tiles cost 10¢ per square cm. How much would it cost to tile an area of .15 m²?

11. Which units (cm², dm², or km²) would you use to measure the area of:

    a) a field?   b)   the cover of a book?   c)   a wall?   d)   a city?

12. Which whole number dimensions for a rectangle with perimeter of 18 cm will give the greatest area?

ME8-29: Surface Area of a Rectangular Prism (Introduction)

1. In each prism, shade **all** the sides that have the same length as the side marked:

   NOTE: Pictures not drawn to scale.

   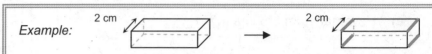

   Example:

   a)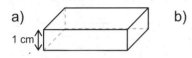

   b)

   c)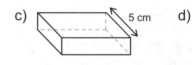

   d)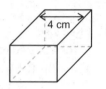

2. Find the missing edge length for each prism:

   a) 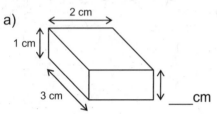 ___ cm

   b) 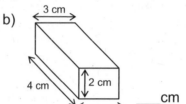 ___ cm

   c) 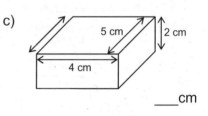 ___ cm

3.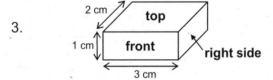

   Show what each face of the box would look like if it was drawn on cm grid paper:

   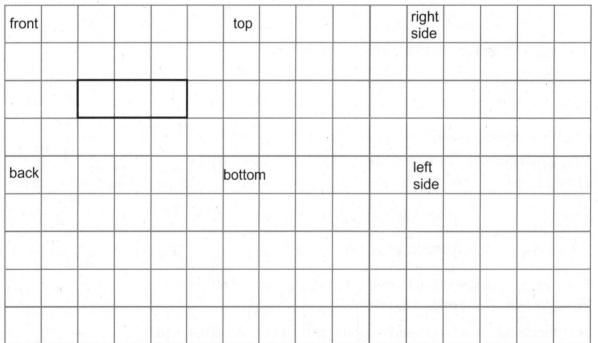

4. Write the area of each face of the box in Question 3:

   front __3 cm²__ back _____ top _____ bottom _____ left side _____ right side _____

5. The **surface area** of a rectangular prism is the total area of all the faces of the prism. What is the surface area of the prism in Question 3? _____

6.   Draw a net for each box. Label each face that shows, as in a):

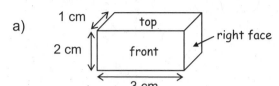

a)   1 cm   top   right face   2 cm   front   3 cm

b)   2 cm   1 cm   4 cm

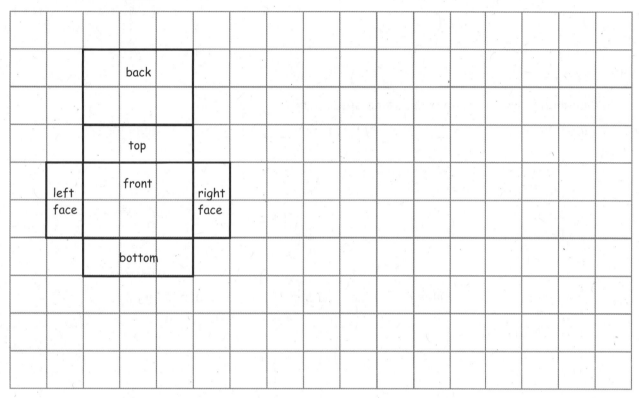

back

top

left face   front   right face

bottom

7.   Write a multiplication statement giving the area of each face for the prisms in question 6. Then write the surface area of the prism:

a)   front __2 × 3 = 6 cm²__   back _____   b)   front _____   back _____

top _____   bottom _____   top _____   bottom _____

right face _____   left face _____   right face _____   left face _____

surface area of prism _____   surface area of prism _____

8.   Draw a net for each prism on cm² grid paper. Then find the surface area of the prism:

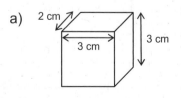

a)   2 cm   3 cm   3 cm

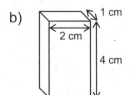

b)   1 cm   2 cm   4 cm

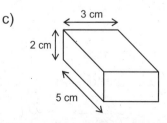

c)   3 cm   2 cm   5 cm

ME8-30: Surface Area of Rectangular Prisms

1. Write the name of each face of the prism on the net. Write the length of each edge on the net (the right face is done for you). Then find the area of each face:

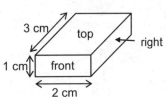

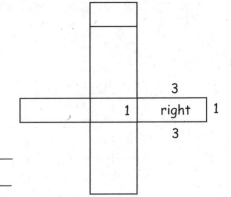

Area:

top _____ cm²   front _____   right _____

bottom _____   back _____   left _____

2. In Question 1, which face has the same area as the ...

   a) top face? _____   b) front face? _____   c) right face? _____

3. Shade the face that has the same area as the shaded face:

   a)   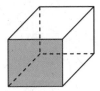   b)   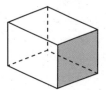   c)

4. The area of each face is written on the face. What is the area of each hidden face?

   a)   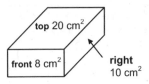   b)   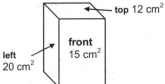   c)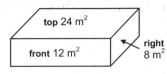

   back _____   back _____   left _____

   bottom _____   bottom _____   bottom _____

   left _____   right _____   back _____

5. Write the area of each visible face directly on the face. Then double each area to find the total area of each pair of congruent faces. Part a) is started for you:

   a)   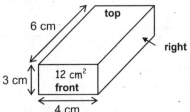   b)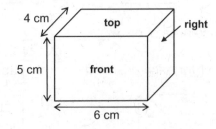

   front + back = ___12 × 2___ = ___24 cm²___   _____

   top + bottom = _____ = _____   _____

   _____ = _____ = _____   _____

Measurement 2

1. Find the surface area of each prism by any method:

a)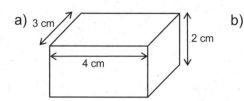

b)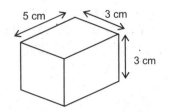

c)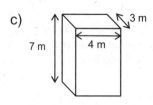

2. Crystal knows that the surface area of the front, top and right faces of a rectangular prism add to 20 cm². How can she find the **total** surface area of the prism? Explain.

_____

_____

3. Sally's teacher tells her that she can find the surface area of the prism by adding the areas of three faces and then multiplying by two. Which of the following will give Sally the right answer? Circle all correct answers:

   i) (area of top + area of bottom + area of right side) × 2   ii) (area of top + area of left side + area of back) × 2

   iii) (area of top + area of right side + area of front) × 2   iv) (area of bottom + area of right side + area of left side) × 2

   v) (area of bottom + area of left side + area of front) × 2   vi) (area of bottom + area of front + area of top) × 2

4. Find the missing length:

a)
3 m | Area = 15 m²
____ m

b)
____ m
5 m | Area = 30 m²

c)
3 m | Area = 21 m²
____ m

5. Find the missing edge length:

a)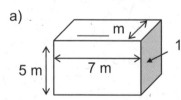

b)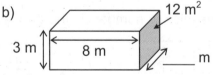

c)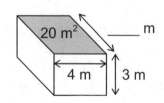

Answer the remaining questions in your notebook.

6. Edges *a*, *b* and *c* have lengths that are whole numbers. The surface area of each face is written directly on the face. What are some possible lengths for edges *a*, *b* and *c*?

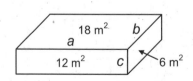

7. Describe two different ways of finding the surface area of a rectangular prism. Which do you prefer?

8. Write a formula for the surface area of the prism using the length (*l*) width (*w*) and height (*h*).

ME8-32: Volume

Volume is the amount of space a three-dimensional (3-D) object occupies.

1 cm³ block

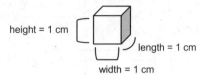

> **NOTE:**
> A 3-D object can be measured in three directions, such as length, width and height.

To measure volume, we use cubic centimetres (cm³):

Example: This object, made of centimetre cubes, has a volume of four cubes – or 4 cubic centimetres (written as 4 cm³):

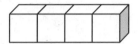

TEACHER: Use centicubes or other materials to construct the models on this page.

- -

1. Using "centicubes" as your unit of measurement, write the <u>volume</u> of each object:

a)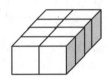

Volume = _____ cubes

b)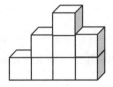

Volume = _____ cubes

c)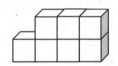

Volume = _____ cubes

d)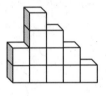

Volume = _____ cubes

e)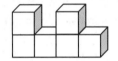

Volume = _____ cubes

f)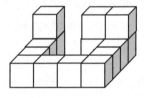

Volume = _____ cubes

2. Given a structure made of cubes, you can draw a top view as shown:

3	1	2
1		

← *The numbers tell you how many cubes are stacked in each position.*

For each figure below, fill in the missing numbers in the top view:

a)

b)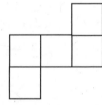

c)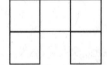

d)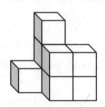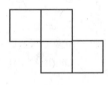

e)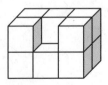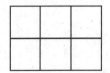

f)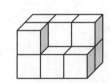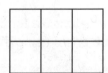

Measurement 2

3. A structure made of cubes each with volume 1 cm³ has this top view:

    What is the volume of the structure? _____

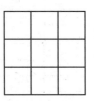

4. This picture shows the top view of a <u>cube</u>. Fill in the missing numbers:

    What is the volume of the cube? _____

    REMEMBER: A cube is as high as it is wide and long.

Answer the following questions in your notebook.

5. On grid paper, draw a top view for each of the following structures (use cubes to help):

a)   b)   c) 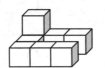   d)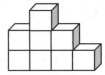

e) 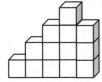   f) 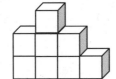   g) 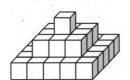   h)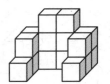

6. Using centicubes, build two different shapes that have the volume of exactly 10 cubic centimetres.
    Draw a top view of each of your shapes.

7. How many different rectangular prisms can you build with 8 cubes?
    Draw a top view for each of your shapes.

8. Given a structure made with cubes, you can draw a front, top and side view as shown:

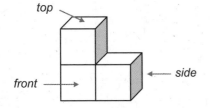

front view: **top view:**   **side view:**

    Draw a front, top and side view for the following structures:
    HINT: Use cubes to help you.

a)   b) 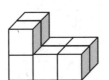   c) 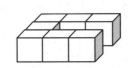   d)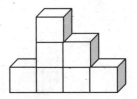

ME8-33: Volume of Rectangular Prisms (Introduction)

1. Use the number of blocks in the shaded column to write an addition statement and a multiplication statement for each area:

   a) 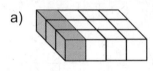   _3_ + _3_ + _3_ + _3_ + = _12_

      _3_ × _4_ = _12_

   b) 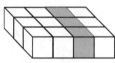   __ + __ + __ + __ + __ = _____

      ___ × ___ = _____

   c) 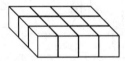   __ + __ + __ + __ + __ + __ + __ = _____

      ___ × ___ = _____

2. How many 1 cm³ blocks are in each shaded row?
   NOTE: Blocks are not shown to scale.

   a)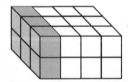

   _____ blocks

   b)

   _____ blocks

   c)

   _____ blocks

   d)

   _____ blocks

3. a) Write an addition statement for the volume of the shape:

      ___ + ___ + ___ + ___ = _____ cm³

   b) Based on your answer in part a), write a multiplication statement for the same volume:

      ___ × ___ = _____ cm³

4.

   a) How many blocks are shaded? _____

   b) Write an addition statement for the volume:

      ____ + ____ + ____ + ____ = _____ cm³

   c) Write a multiplication statement for the same volume: ____ × 4 = _____ cm³

5. Write an addition or multiplication statement for each volume:

   a)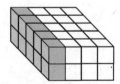

      ____ + ____ + ____ = _____ cm³

      ____ × _3_ = _____ cm³

   b)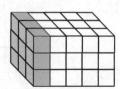

      ____ + ____ + ____ + ____ = _____ cm³

      ____ × ____ = _____ cm³

   c)

      ____ + ____ + ____ + ____ + ____ = _____ cm³

      ____ × ____ = _____ cm³

6. Write a multiplication statement for the total volume of the rectangular prism by first counting the number of 1 cm³ blocks that are shaded:

a)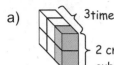

$$\underline{2\ cm^3} \times \underline{\ 3\ } = \underline{\ 6\ }\ cm^3$$

b)

blocks in   number
each row   of rows

$$\underline{2\ cm^3} \times \underline{\ 3\ } \times \underline{\ 2\ } = 12\ cm^3$$

c)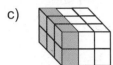

$$2\ cm^3 \times 3 \times \underline{\ \ \ } = \underline{\ \ \ \ }\ cm^3$$

d)

$$2\ cm^3 \times 3 \times \underline{\ \ \ } = \underline{\ \ \ \ }\ cm^3$$

e)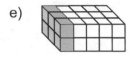

$$2\ cm^3 \times 3 \times \underline{\ \ \ } = \underline{\ \ \ \ }\ cm^3$$

f)

$$3\ cm^3 \times 3 \times \underline{\ \ \ } = \underline{\ \ \ \ }\ cm^3$$

$3\ cm^3 \times 3$

7. Find the surface area of the left-most layer:

a)

surface area:

$$= \underline{\ \ \ }\ cm \times \underline{\ \ \ }\ cm = \underline{\ \ \ }\ cm^2$$

b)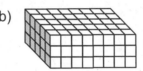

surface area:

$$= \underline{\ \ \ }\ cm \times \underline{\ \ \ }\ cm = \underline{\ \ \ }\ cm^2$$

c)

surface area"

$$= \underline{\ \ \ }\ cm \times \underline{\ \ \ }\ cm = \underline{\ \ \ }\ cm^2$$

8. For each prism in Question 7, find the volume of the left-most layer of blocks:

a) $\underline{\ \ \ \ }\ cm^3$ b) $\underline{\ \ \ \ }\ cm^3$ c) $\underline{\ \ \ \ }\ cm^3$

9. For each prism in Question 7, compare the surface area and the volume of the left-most layer. Are the numbers the same or different? _____

10. Each edge in a 1 cm³ block is 1 cm long:

1 cm

layer

a)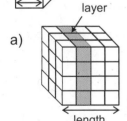

number of layers = _____

length of side = _____

b)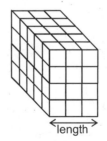

number of layers = _____

length of side = _____

length

11. Compare the **length** of each prism in Question 10 with the **number of layers**. Are the numbers the same or different? _____

12. The volume of a right rectangular prism made of cm³ cubes is: (number of layers in prism) × (number of cubes in each layer). In your notebook, explain why this formula gives the same answer as (length of prism) × (surface area of left face of prism).

ME8-34: Surface Area and Volume

1. Find the volume of each prism by multiplying the surface area of the left face by the length:

a)

b)

c)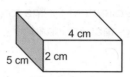

d)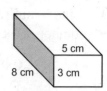

Left surface area	Left surface area	Left surface area	Left surface area
= _____ cm²	= _____ cm²	= _____ cm²	= _____ cm²
Length = ____ cm	Length = ____ cm	Length = ____ cm	Length = ____ cm
Volume = ___ cm³	Volume = ___ cm³	Volume = ___ cm³	Volume = ___ cm³

2. Write a multiplication statement for each volume by counting the number of 1 cm³ blocks:

a)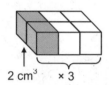

b)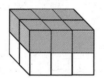

c)

d)

a) 2 cm³ × __3__

= __6__ cm³

b) 2 cm³ × 3 × ____

= ____ cm³

c) 2 cm³ × 3 × ____

= ____ cm³

d) 2 cm³ × 3 × ____

= ____ cm³

3. a) Look at each rectangular prism from Question 2. Complete the following chart:

Shape	Surface area of top	Height	Volume
A			
B			
C			
D			

b) Say how to calculate the volume of a rectangular prism from the surface area of the top layer and the height of the prism:

4. A rectangular prism has length *l*, width *w* and height *h*:

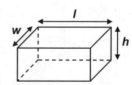

a) Write a formula for the surface area of the top (using *l* and *w*): _____

b) Write a formula for the volume of the prism (using *l*, *w* and *h*) : _____

Measurement 2

5. Complete the following statements by using the words **length**, **width** and **height**:

    In a right-rectangular prism…

    a)   … the surface area of the top × <u>height</u> = volume

    b)   … the surface area of the right side × _____ = volume

    c)   … the surface area of the bottom × _____ = volume

    d)   … the surface area of the back × _____ = volume

    e)   … the surface area of the left side × _____ = volume

    f)   … the surface area of the front × _____ = volume

    g)   … the surface area of the top = _____ × _____

    h)   … from a) and g), the volume is: _____ × _____ × _____

6. Find the volume of each right rectangular prism. Include the units in your answer:

    a)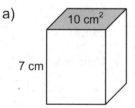

    b)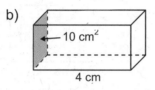

    c)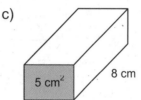

    d)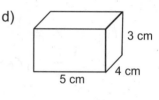

Answer the following questions in your notebook.

7. Write one possible set of lengths, widths and heights for a rectangular prism with volume.

    a) 12 cm^3 b) 8 cm^3 c) 18 m^3

8. The area of the base of a right rectangle prism is 8 cm^2 and its volume is 32 cm^3. What is its height?

9. Find the length and width of all rectangles with perimeter twelve (and sides with lengths that are whole numbers). Which rectangle has the least area?

10. The volume of a rectangular prism is 24 cm^3 and its height is 2 cm. What can be the dimensions of the base of the prism?

11. Find 3 possible lengths, widths and heights in a rectangular prism with volume 24 cm^3. Which one would require the least amount of material to construct?

12. The picture shows the top view of a rectangular prism made of cm^3:

    a)   What is its surface area in cm^2?

    b)   What is its volume in cm^3?

3	3	3
3	3	3

13. a)   Write a rule that tells you how to calculate the surface area of the figures from the figure number (each cube has length, width and height 1 cm)

    b)   Use your rule to predict the surface area of the 20th figure.

Figure 1   **Figure 2**   **Figure 3**

1. Find the volumes of the rectangular prisms from the top views shown below:

a)

5	5	5
5	5	5

Width: _____

Length: _____

Height: _____

Volume = _____

b)

3	3
3	3

Width: _____

Length: _____

Height: _____

Volume = _____

c)

2	2	2	2	2
2	2	2	2	2

Width: _____

Length: _____

Height: _____

Volume = _____

2. Find the volume of each box with the indicated dimensions (assume all units are in metres):

    HINT: V = H × L × W

a)

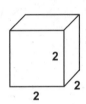

Width: _____

Length: _____

Height: _____

Volume = _____

b)

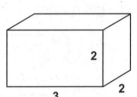

Width: _____

Length: _____

Height: _____

Volume = _____

c)

Width: _____

Length: _____

Height: _____

Volume = _____

d)

Width: _____

Length: _____

Height: _____

Volume = _____

3. Find all the possible lengths, widths and heights for a box with the given volume so that the measurements are in whole numbers:

    HINT: There are 6 possibilities for part b).

a) Volume = 3 cm^3

Height	Width	Length

b) Volume = 4 cm^3

Height	Width	Length

4. In your notebook, draw the top view of a rectangular prism with the given dimensions. Then calculate the volume:

a) Width 3 cm; Length 4 cm; Height 5 cm

b) Width 4 cm; Height 4 cm; Length 19 cm

ME8-36: Volume of Triangular Prisms

1. a) What fraction of the rectangle is shaded? _____

   b) What is the area of the rectangle in square units? _____

   c) What is the area of the shaded part? _____

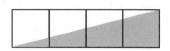

2. a) What fraction of the volume of each rectangular prism (r.p.) below is the volume of the triangular prism (t.p.)? _____

   b) What would you divide the volume of each rectanglular prism to find the volume of the t.p.?

   _____

   c) Fill in the blanks:

   i)
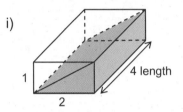

   ii)
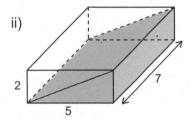

   iii)
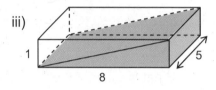

   volume of r.p. = _____   volume of r.p. = _____   volume of r.p. = _____

   volume of t.p. = _____   volume of t.p. = _____   volume of t.p. = _____

3. Recall that the area of a triangle is: $\frac{1}{2}$ × base × height   *or*   (base × height) ÷ 2

   a) Look at the triangular prisms in Question 2 c). Calculate the area of each triangular base:

   i)

   ii)

   iii)
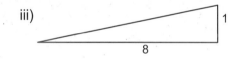

   Area of   Area of   Area of
   triangular   triangular   triangular
   base = _____   base = _____   base = _____

   b) Multiply the area of each triangular base by the length of the prism:

   i)
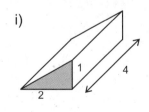

   ii)
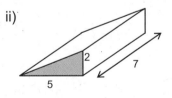

   iii)
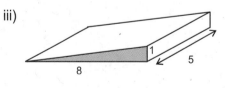

   _____ × _____   _____ × _____   _____ × _____
   Area of base   Length   Area of base   Length   Area of base   Length

   c) Compare the numbers you calculated in Question 3 b) i), ii), iii) with the volumes of the r.t.p. you calculated in Question 2 c) i), ii), iii).
      What do you notice?

jump math
MULTIPLYING POTENTIAL.

Measurement 2

ME8-36: Volume of Triangular Prisms *(continued)*

4. You can divide any triangle into two right triangles.

   What fraction of the area of the rectangle is the triangle? _____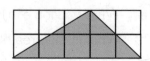

   HINT: Divide the rectangle into 2 smaller rectangles that contain the right triangles. What fraction of the area of each smaller rectangle is the right triangle?

5.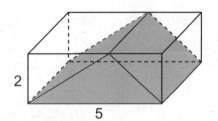

   What fraction of the r.p. is the t.p.? _____

   HINT: You can divide the r.p. into two smaller t.p.

6. Find the volume of each r.p., then the volume of t.p.:

   a)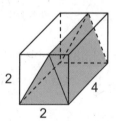

   fraction shaded _____
   volume of r.p. _____
   volume of t.p. _____

   b)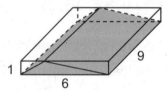

   fraction shaded _____
   volume of r.p. _____
   volume of t.p. _____

   c)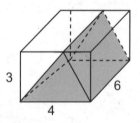

   fraction shaded _____
   volume of r.p. _____
   volume of t.p. _____

   d)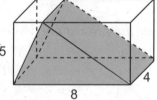

   fraction shaded _____
   volume of r.p. _____
   volume of t.p. _____

BONUS:

7. Find the surface area of the figure in Question 6 a).

ME8-37: Changing Units of Volume

1. Each of the small cubes in Figure 1 has sides 1 cm and volume 1 cm^3 (not drawn to scale).

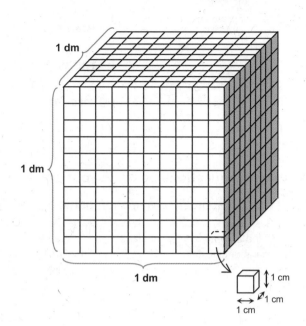

   a) How many 1 cm^3 cubes cover the front layer of the large cube? _____

   b) How many 1 cm^3 cubes fit into the large cube?
   _____

   c) What is the volume of the large cube in cm^3?
   _____

   d) How long are the sides of the large square in dm? _____

   e) A dm^3 is _____ times larger than a cm^3.

Answer the following questions in your notebook.

2. Follow the steps in part a) to answer each question:

   a) Change 27 000 cm^3 to dm^3.
      The new units are **1000** times **bigger**.
      So **divide** by **1000**.
      So 27 000 cm^3 = 27 dm^3

   b) Change 370 cm^3 to dm^3.
   c) Change 29 dm^3 to cm^3.
   d) Change .53 dm^3 to cm^3.
   e) Change 1.4 cm^3 to dm^3.

3. Ken says 1 m^3 = 10 dm × 10 dm × 10 dm.
   So 10 × 10 × 10 = 1000 dm^3 will fit into 1 m^3.

   Use Ken's reasoning to fill in the blanks below:

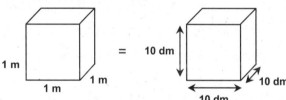

a)

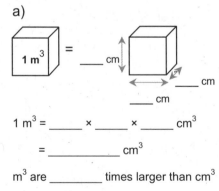

1 m^3 = _____ × _____ × _____ cm^3

   = _____ cm^3

m^3 are _____ times larger than cm^3

b)

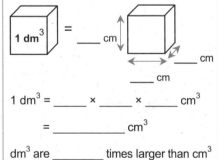

1 dm^3 = _____ × _____ × _____ cm^3

   = _____ cm^3

dm^3 are _____ times larger than cm^3

c)

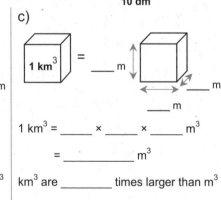

1 km^3 = _____ × _____ × _____ m^3

   = _____ m^3

km^3 are _____ times larger than m^3

4. Change the following units. Parts k) to p) are challenging:

   a) 2 m^3 to dm^3
   b) 40 000 dm^3 to m^3
   c) 52 cm^3 to dm^3
   d) 7 dm^3 to cm^3
   e) 72 365 dm^3 to m^3
   f) 2342 cm^3 to m^3
   g) 8 cm^3 to dm^3
   h) 3.7 dm^3 to cm^3
   i) 2400 cm^3 to m^3
   j) .000 001 m^3 to cm^3
   k) 4 km^3 to m^3
   l) 2 736 254 m^3 to km^3
   m) 5.2 dm^3 to mm^3
   n) 3.85 m^3 to mm^3
   o) .02 m^3 to mm^3
   p) 174 mm^3 to m^3

ME8-38: Circumference

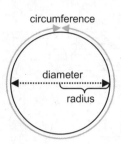

The **diameter** of a circle is the distance across the circle.

The **radius** is half the diameter.

The **circumference** is the distance around the circle.

Answer the questions below in your notebook.

1. Find the approximate relation between the diameter and circumference of a circle as follows:

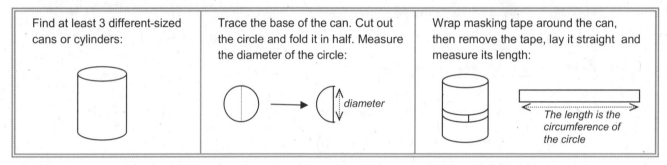

Find at least 3 different-sized cans or cylinders:	Trace the base of the can. Cut out the circle and fold it in half. Measure the diameter of the circle:	Wrap masking tape around the can, then remove the tape, lay it straight and measure its length:

You will find that the circumference of the circle is always about 3 times the diameter.

To find the circumference of a circle you can always multiply the diameter by a fixed number "pi" (π). The value of π is approximately 3.14.

Circumference = $\pi \times$ diameter *or* **Circumference = $2\pi \times$ radius**

Find the approximate circumference of circles with the given measurements (use 3.14 for π):

a) diameter = 10 m   b) diameter = 7 m   c) diameter = 6 cm   d) radius = 4 m   e) radius = 2.5 cm

2. Find the approximate circumference of each coin (use 3 for π):

a)   a dime with diameter 18 mm   b)   a quarter with diameter 24 mm

BONUS:

3. Find the perimeter of each figure:

a)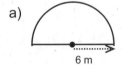
6 m

b)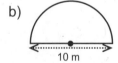
10 m

c)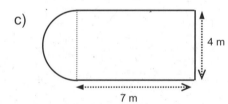
4 m
7 m

4. A race track consists of a rectangle and two semi-circles, as shown:

a)   How far does the inside runner have to run?

b)   How far does the outside runner (running on the dotted line) have to run?

c)   How much of a head start should the outside runner be given?

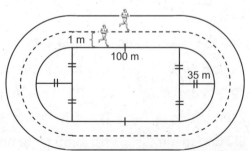
1 m
100 m
35 m

 jump math
MULTIPLYING POTENTIAL

Measurement 2

1. To find the approximate relation between the
    radius of a circle and its <u>area</u>, try the following
    exercise:

    Draw a circle with a compass. Cut out the circle and fold
    it in half 3 times:

    Figure 1

    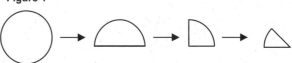

    Cut along the fold lines of the circle and rearrange the
    pieces as shown:

    Figure 2

    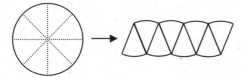

    You can draw a parallelogram around the shape you
    made. The area of the parallelogram is <u>almost</u> equal to
    the area of the circle:

    Figure 3

    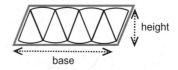

    a) Is the <u>height</u> of the parallelogram in Figure 3 approximately equal to the <u>radius</u> of the circle or
        the <u>diameter</u> of the circle? _____

    b) Is the <u>base</u> of the parallelogram approximately equal to the <u>circumference</u> of the circle or <u>half
        the circumference</u> of the circle? _____

    c) The formula for the area of a parallelogram is Area = base × height. Use your answer for parts
        a) and b) to give the approximate area of the parallelogram:

        Area of parallelogram ≈ _____ × _____

                                        approximate height   approximate base
                                        of parallelogram   of parallelogram

2. The correct answer for Question 1 c) is:

        Area of parallelogram ≈ radius of circle × $\frac{1}{2}$ the circumference of circle

    Since the circumference of a circle of radius r is 2πr:

        Area of parallelogram ≈ $r \times \frac{1}{2} \times 2\pi r$

    But since $\frac{1}{2} \times 2 = 1$:

        Area of parallelogram ≈ _r_ × _πr_ = πr^2

    The area of the parallelogram is approximately equal to the area of the circle.
    Mathematicians have shown that the <u>actual</u> area of a circle is given by the formula: πr^2.
    Use the formula above to find the area of the circles with the given dimensions:

    a) radius: 3 m   b) radius: 5 cm   c) radius: 10 km   d) radius: 7 m

        Area = _____   Area = _____   Area = _____   Area = _____

3. What is the area of a circle with diameter:

    a) 12 m   b) 34 cm   c) 30 dm

        Area = _____   Area = _____   Area = _____

Answer the questions below in your notebook.

4. Find the area and circumference (or perimeter) of each figure.

a)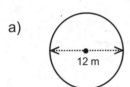

b)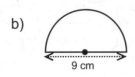

c)

d)

5. 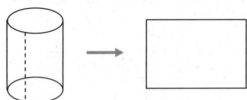 A soup can has its top and bottom removed. The diameter of the can is 6 cm and the height is 10 cm. Find the perimeter of the rectangle obtained by cutting along the dotted line.

6. A rotating water sprinkler can spray water a distance of 20 m. What area of grass can the sprinkler cover?

BONUS:

7. What is the area of the shaded region?

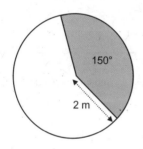

8. The length of each arrow is 1 cm. What is the area of the shaded region?

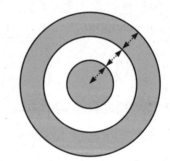

9. Find the area of each shaded region.

a)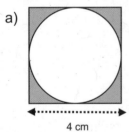

b)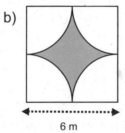

c)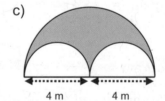

d)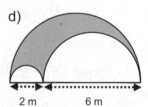

10. Find the perimeter of the shaded regions in Question 9 b) and c).

11. A tractor wheel has diameter 1 metre. About how many times would the wheel turn if the tractor drove 100 m?

ME8-40: Surface Area of a Cylinder

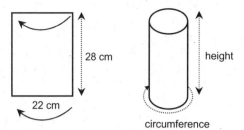

Answer the following questions in your notebook.

1. Take a standard 22 cm by 28 cm sheet of paper and fold it to form a tube.

   a) What is the height of the cylinder?

   b) What is the circumference of the circular base?

2. A paper towel tube can be cut and unwrapped to form a rectangle.

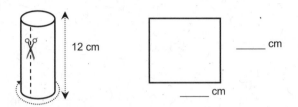

   _____ cm

   _____ cm

   a) Fill in the length and width of the rectangle.

   b) Find the area of the rectangle.

   c) What is the surface area of the tube?

3. Find the surface area of each tube by finding the length and width of a rectangle with the same area.

   a)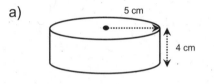

   b)

   c)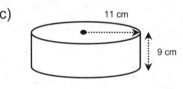

4. Write a formula for the surface area (SA) of a tube in terms of…

   a) the circumference of the circular base and the height: SA = _____

   b) the diameter of the circular base and the height: SA = _____

   c) the radius of the circular base and the height: SA = _____

5. A can of food has a label. The label can be unwrapped to form a rectangle:

   Area of rectangle   = _____

   Area of top circle   = _____

   Area of bottom circle   = _____

   Surface area of can   = _____

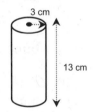

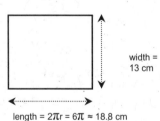

   width = 13 cm

   length = $2\pi r = 6\pi \approx 18.8$ cm

6. Find the surface area of each can by first finding:
   i) the area of a rectangle   ii) the area of the top and bottom circles

   a)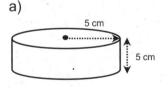

   b)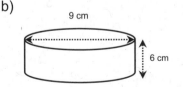

   c)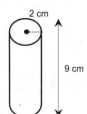

7. A cylindrical can has a circular base of radius r and a height h.
   Write down a formula for its surface area. Don't forget to include the top and bottom.

Measurement 2

1. Calculate the volume of each right prism:

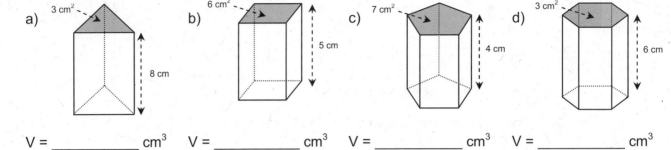

a) V = _____ cm³   b) V = _____ cm³   c) V = _____ cm³   d) V = _____ cm³

2. In your notebook, predict a formula for the volume of a cylinder in terms of its base and height. Explain your prediction.

3. The volume of a cylinder is equal to its (area of base) × height. Find the volume of each cylinder:

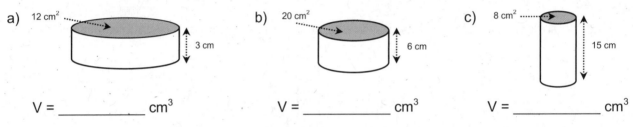

a) V = _____ cm³   b) V = _____ cm³   c) V = _____ cm³

4. Use the radius or diameter to find the area of the base and the volume of the cylinder:

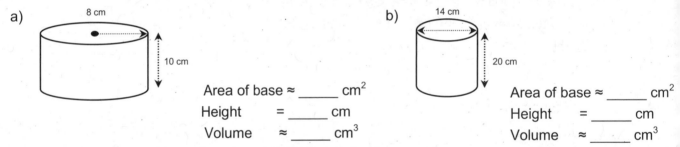

a)

Area of base ≈ _____ cm²
Height   = _____ cm
Volume   ≈ _____ cm³

b)

Area of base ≈ _____ cm²
Height   = _____ cm
Volume   ≈ _____ cm³

Answer the remaining questions in your notebook.

5. Tina has a 20 cm high cylindrical jar. She can fit 30 candies flat on the bottom of the jar. If each candy is 1 cm high, how many candies can she fit into the jar?

6. Satya has two containers, as shown:

   a) Calculate the volume of each container.
      Which one will hold more?

   b) How could Satya check which container will hold more without first finding the volume of each?

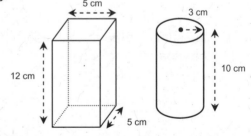

7. a) A prism is made with a 10 cm by 10 cm square base. A cylinder is made so that its base has equal area to the square based prism. Find the radius of the cylinder.

   b) If both are 20 cm high, which container will use less material to make?

   c) Do both containers have the same volume? Explain.

Measurement 2

Answer the following questions in your notebook.

1. The base of a can of concentrated orange juice is a circle with diameter 6.8 cm. The height of the can is 12.2 cm.
   a) Find the volume of the can.
   b) To make orange juice, you add 3 cans of water to the concentrate.
      How much juice (in L) will you have?

2. A can of juice concentrate has diameter 6.8 cm. The label is 12 cm high. There is a 5 mm overlap on the label. What is the area of the label?

3. Each square is 3 cm by 3 cm

   a) Find the area of the large circle:
   b) Find the area of the nine small circles.
   c) Find the area of the shaded region in each square.

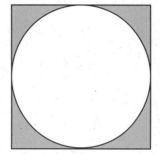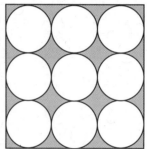

4. A triangle has base equal to the circumference of a circle of radius 3 cm and area equal to the area of the circle. Find the height of the triangle.

5. a) Find the surface area of the interior of the room excluding the door.
   b) It costs $0.40 per square metre to paint a room. How much would it cost to paint the room (excluding the door)?

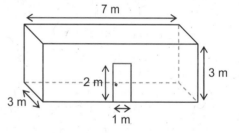

6. Find the volume of the shape:

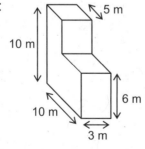

7. The two containers shown hold the same amount of pea soup.

   a) How tall is the second container?
   b) Find the surface area of each container.
   c) It cost 8 ¢ for each cm² of metal to build a can. How much will it cost to make each can? Which can is cheaper?

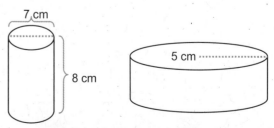

PDM8-17: Mean, Median and Mode

1. Re-write the data in order from lowest to highest, then find the range:

   a) 37 21 43 59 6

      6 21 37 43 59

      range: __59 – 6 = 53__

   b) 8 105 43 81 65 34 298

      _____

      range: _____

   c) 58 53 56 722 587 404 23

      _____

      range: _____

   d) 58 55 55 56 54 57

      _____

      range: _____

2. To find the mean, add the values and divide by the total number of values:

   a) 4 9 7 2 6 8

      _4_ + _9_ + _7_ + _2_ + _6_ + _8_ = _36_

      _36_ ÷ _6_ = _6_ mean: _6_

   b) 3 10 6 4 7

      ___ + ___ + ___ + ___ + ___ = ___

      _____ ÷ _____ = _____ mean: _____

   c) 4 5 2 2 8 9

      ___ + ___ + ___ + ___ + ___ + ___ = ___

      _____ ÷ _____ = _____ mean: _____

   d) 12 11 5 6 4 4 0

      ___ + ___ + ___ + ___ + ___ + ___ + ___ = ___

      _____ ÷ _____ = _____ mean: _____

3. Find the mode:

The **mode** is the number that appears the most often.

   a) 14 21 18 16 14 13 11 mode: __14__

   b) 8 2 2 mode: _____

   c) 18 35 18 54 mode: _____

   d) 12 53 72 13 53 35 mode: _____

   e) 6 6 3 5 3 8 10 6 2 5 3 3 6 4 8 6 mode: _____

To find the median of a data set, put the data in order and then count from either end until you reach the middle	2 3 6 ⑦ 9 11 15 ↑ ↑ ↑ ↑ ↑ ↑ 1 2 3 3 2 1 The median is 7	If there are 2 middle numbers, the median is the mean of these two numbers.

4. Write each data set in order from lowest to highest and then find the median:

   a) 13 9 14 12 11

      _____

      median: _____

   b) 41 15 43 44 29 64

      _____

      median: _____

   c) 71 58 12 13 71 65 12 48

      _____

      median: _____

5. Find the mean, mode and median:

   a) 1 1 1

      mean: _____ mode: _____

      median: _____

   b) 3 3 3 3 3

      mean: _____ mode: _____

      median: _____

   c) 14 14 14 14 14

      mean: _____ mode: _____

      median: _____

6. When all the values in a data set are the same, what are the mean, mode and median?

   _____

TEACHER: Students should answer these exercises in their notebooks. They will need square tiles that they can arrange in columns or "stacks". If you don't have tiles, students should draw the stacks on grid paper.

1. Shawn makes a model of the data set 3, 5, 6, 8, 8 using stacks of square tiles. To find the mean, he rearranges the stacks so that each stack has the same number of blocks.

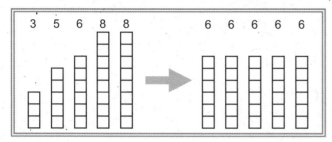

a) What is the mean of the set of values 3 5 6 8 8?

_____

b) Does rearranging the stacks change

   i)   the number of blocks? ___

   ii)   the number of data values? ____

   iii)   The mean? ____

2. Find the mean of each data set by stacking blocks and then rearranging stacks:

a) 3 7 6 4

   mean: ____

b) 5 10 6 6 8

   mean: ____

c) 2 2 2 2 17

   mean: ____

You can't always rearrange the stacks so that each stack has the same number of blocks, but the mean may be easier to estimate.

Example: 3 5 6 8 9   6 6 6 6 7

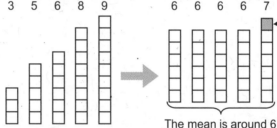

The mean is around 6

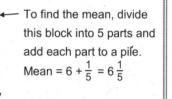

To find the mean, divide this block into 5 parts and add each part to a pile.

Mean $= 6 + \frac{1}{5} = 6\frac{1}{5}$

3. Rearrange stacks to help estimate the mean. Then calculate the mean:

a) 5 10 6 8 9

b) 4 3 6 7 2 5

c) 3 6 7 8 4 2 2 5

4. Find each missing value using blocks **and** the formula:

   RECALL: Mean = (sum of data values) ÷ (number of data values)

a) 1 3 7 4 5

   sum of data values: __20__

   number of data values: _5_

   mean: __4__

   (mean) × (number of data values) : __20__

b) 2 9 6 11

   sum of data values: _____

   number of data values: ___

   mean: _____

   (mean) × (number of data values) : _____

c) 1 4 2 3 5 3

   sum of data values: _____

   number of data values: ___

   mean: _____

   (mean) × (number of data values) : _____

5. What number is equal to (mean) × (number of data values)? Explain in your notebook.

6. In each case, find the sum of the data values:

a) mean: 6

   number of data values: 7

   sum of data values: __42__

b) mean: 13

   number of data values: 3

   sum of data values: _____

c) mean: 6

   number of data values: 20

   sum of data values: _____

PDM8-19: Exploring the Mean, Median and Mode (Advanced)

1. Use blocks to create a data set with 5 data values, mean 4 and …

   HINT: The number of blocks is: sum of the data values = mean × (number of data values)

   a) mode 6 _____ _____ _____ _____ _____

   b) interval 3 – 7 _____ _____ _____ _____ _____

   c) mode 2 _____ _____ _____ _____ _____

   d) median 3 _____ _____ _____ _____ _____

2. Use blocks to create a data set with 4 data values, mean 6 and …

   a) mode 5, interval 4 – 10 _____

   b) mode 6, median 6 _____

   c) interval 3 – 11, median 5 _____

   d) mode 5, interval 5 – 8 _____

3. For each set of values below, either find a data set with these values or state that it is not possible. Use blocks if it helps:

   a) 5 data values, mean 4, interval 2 – 4 _____

   b) 5 data values, mean 3, interval 0 – 4 _____

   c) 3 data values, mean 4, mode 5, interval 3 – 5 _____

4. In each case find the missing data value. **HINT: Sum of data values = mean × (number of data values).**

   a) 3 7 9 4 ___7___

   mean = 6

   sum of data values

   = _6 × 5 = 30_

   missing value

   = _30 – (3 + 7 + 9 + 4)_

   = _30 – 23 = 7_

   b) 6 4 _____

   mean = 7

   sum of data values

   = _____

   missing value

   = _____

   = _____

   c) 1 2 3 _____

   mean = 3

   sum of data values

   = _____

   missing value

   = _____

   = _____

5. In each case, the mean is 80. Find the missing value:

   a) 80 _____

   b) 78 _____

   c) 78 78 _____

   d) 75 81 79 80 _____

6. After 2 tests, Safara's average (mean) was 80%.

   a) What was her mark on the second test if …

   i) She got 80 on the first? _____   ii) She got 78 on the first? _____   iii) She got 90 on the first? _____

   b) If the mode was 80, what were the two marks? _____

   c) If the highest mark was 20 more than the lowest mark, what were the two marks? _____

7. Sally has 82 81 84 83 on the first 4 tests.

   a) She wants to average 85 on her 5 tests. What does she need on the 5th test?

   b) Would it be possible for her to average 90 on all 5 tests? Why or why not? _____

   _____

8. How many blocks would you need to build a data set with…

   a) 4 data values and mean 5? _____

   b) 5 data values and mean 4? _____

   c) 5 data values and mean 6? _____

   d) 10 data values and mean 13? _____

PDM8-20: Using the Mean, Median and Mode

1. Use a calculator (or computer) to find:

a) 9 20 22

mean __17__ median __20__

b) 18 20 22

mean ____ median ____

c) 10 15 20 25 30

mean ____ median ____

d) 15 18 20 32 40

mean ____ median ____

e) 15 16 17 21 22 27 29

mean ____ median ____

f) 10 15 20 25 40

mean ____ median ____

2. The data from Question 1 is shown. Circle the data sets that look symmetrical around the median:

a)
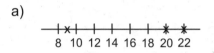

b)
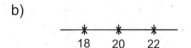

c)
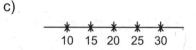

d)
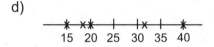

e)

f)

3. Look at your answers to Questions 1 and 2. Does the data that looks symmetrical tend to have mean and median that are:
   ➢ close together, or
   ➢ far apart?

4. You work at a clothing store and your manager says that every week you need an average daily sales of at least $500. Do you think the manager means "mode", "median" or "mean" by the word "average"? Why?

5. A store owner is deciding what size of shoes to order. He looks at his data.

Shoe Size	5	6	7	8	9	10	11	12
Number Sold	2	12	35	28	20	9	4	1

How many shoes did he sell altogether? To decide what size of shoes to order, which is most important? Mean, median or mode? Why?

6. a) Use blocks to find a set of 5 test scores ranging from 2 to 7 with mean 5, median 5 and mode 7.

   b) Add a test score of 12 to your data set from part a). How does this affect the range, the mean, the mode and the median?
   REMEMBER: When finding the mean and the median, there is now one more data value.

   range = _____   mean = _____   mode = _____   median = _____

7. You are planning a vacation in March Break and need to know what kind of clothes to take with you. The chart below shows, for last year's March Break, the highest daily temperatures in the place you are going to visit:

Day	1	2	3	4	5	6	7	8	9	10	11	12	13	14	15
°C	23	22	20	21	22	23	23	10	2	2	5	7	8	12	17

a) Temperature range is _____, mean = _____, mode = _____, median = _____.

b) If you looked only at the mode of the temperatures, what mistake might you make in your packing?

c) Which measure (mean, median or mode) is most useful for your planning? Why?

8. True or False:

a) The mode gives the item occurring most often.   T   F

b) The mean must be a member of the data set.   T   F

c) The mode must be a member of the data set.   T   F

d) The median must be a member of the data set.   T   F

e) The mode is easy to read from a bar graph.   T   F

f) The mean gives the middle number.   T   F

g) In a data set of 2 pieces of data, the mean and median are the same.   T   F

9. Give an example of a data set where…

a) The mode is also the largest value:

b) The mean is the smallest value:

c) The mean is the median, but not the mode:

d) The median is the mode, but not the mean:

Answer the remaining questions in your notebook.

10. You have 6 whole number data values. Find the lowest possible sum of all values if…
    NOTE: Zero is a possible data value.

    a) the median is 500.   b) the mean is 500.   c) the mode is 500.

11. When a soccer player moved from Team A to Team B, the mean age of **both** teams increased. Give an example of data to show how this could happen.

12. When finding the median, does it matter whether you write the data list from lowest to highest, or from highest to lowest?

13. Find a data set, not all numbers equal, where the mean, mode and median are all equal.
    HINT: Guess and check.

If you collect information by surveying an entire population, you are using a **census**.

If you only survey a part of the population, you are using a **sample**.

Answer the questions below in your notebook.

1. Would you use a sample or a census to find out …

   a) … which movie your 5 friends want to watch?

   b) … who your school thinks should be school president?

   c) … how smoking affects people's lungs?

   d) … whether people in your home city would support an NHL team if the NHL wanted to expand?

2. The principal of a school wants to find out if students think that school should start and finish half an hour earlier, but he doesn't have time to ask everyone. He does two surveys:

   A: He asks the first 50 students who arrive in the morning. YES 40 NO 10
   B: He asks 5 students from each of the ten classrooms. YES 20 NO 30

   a) Why didn't the two surveys get the same results?

   b) Which group's opinion will be most similar to the whole school's opinion?

   c) If there are 500 people in the school, how many do you think will want school to start and finish half an hour earlier?

   > *A* **representative sample** *is similar to the whole population. A* **biased sample** *is not similar to the whole population because some parts are not represented. When teachers ask only the first 50 students who arrive whether or not they want school to start and finish earlier, they are only asking students who find it convenient to come in early.*

3. Decide whether each sample is biased or representative. Explain the cause of any bias.

   a) On a weekend, a model airplane club tests two plane designs to see how long they can remain in the air.

   - On each day, they test 5 planes of each design. <u>**Representative**</u>
   - On the first day, they test 10 planes of one design and on the second day, they test 10 planes of the other design. <u>**Biased**</u>
   - On one day, it might be windier, causing the planes to stay in the air longer on one day than on another day. The conditions are different on the two days, so the sample is **biased.**

b) A grade 1-8 school is planning a party and they want to have board games available. To find out which board games are the most popular, they ask:

- 40 grade 7 and 8 students
- 5 students from each grade

c) A health team is comparing the heart rate of 15-year-olds before and after a half hour of exercise. They test the heart rate of:

- 25 members of a school track and field team
- 25 students from a class

d) A class is testing two brands of seeds to find out what percent will germinate. They plant:

- 10 seeds from each package
- The 10 largest seeds from each package

e) Students want to know if they're faster at doing multiplication by 2 or by 5.

- The whole class does 20 multiplications by 2 and then 20 by 5.
- Half the class multiplies by 2 first and then by 5; the other half multiplies by 5 first and then 2.

4. A city wants to build either a new hockey arena, a new swimming pool or a new library. Which of the following places is the best site for a survey?

- A beach
- A bookstore
- A professional hockey game
- A shopping mall

Why? What's wrong with the other three?

5. Two students, Katie and Melanie are running for student elections. They want to know how many of the school's 250 students will vote for them.

- Katie asks the 25 students in her class and finds that 15 will vote for her and 10 will not.
- Melanie gets a student list from the principal and asks every tenth student on the list. She finds that 15 will vote for her and 10 will not.

Whose sample is more biased? Why?
Who do you think will win the election? Why?

PDM8-22: Designing, Displaying and Analysing a Survey

Now it's your turn to do a survey.

Record all of your ideas, data, observations and conclusions in your notebook.

1. A survey usually asks a particular question, for example:
   How do you get to school? What is your favourite colour?
   How big is your family?

   Ask yourself: *What question will my survey ask?*

2. It is sometimes a good idea to offer people a sample of possible answers, for instance:
   Do you walk to school or do you take the bus?

   Ask yourself: *What responses do I expect? Do I need to include an "other" category?*

3. You should pick a representative group and be sure to include enough people in your survey. If you wanted to find out which sports students in your school prefer, you wouldn't only ask people in one grade. And you would ask more than one or two people!

   Ask yourself: *Who should I survey? How many people should I survey?*

4. Before conducting your survey, try to predict the results.
   What answer do you think will be the most common? The least common?

   Ask yourself: *What are my predicted results?*

5. Next, you'll need to create a tally sheet to keep track of the responses you'll get. For example:

How do you get to school?	Tally
Walk	
Take the bus	
Ride my bike	

6. Now that you have collected your survey data, you need to display it.

   Ask yourself: *Would I prefer to use a bar graph, a line graph or pie chart? What scale should I use?*
   NOTE: Don't forget to label everything clearly and include a descriptive title.

7. Finally, you should use your results to draw conclusions about your survey.

   Ask yourself: What results did I get? Would it be useful to analyze my data (e.g. find the mean, median, mode or range)? What would this tell me? Did people respond as I'd expected? Was there a trend in my data? Did I learn anything interesting from my survey?

jump math
MULTIPLYING POTENTIAL

Probability & Data Management 2

The different ways an event can happen are called **outcomes** of the event.

When Alice plays a game of cards with a friend, there are three possible outcomes: (1) Alice wins, (2) Alice loses or (3) the game ends without a winner or a loser (this is sometimes called a tie or a draw).

REMEMBER: **A coin has two sides:** **A die has six sides,**
heads and tails. **numbered 1 to 6.**

- -

1. What are the possible outcomes when:

   a) You flip a coin? _____

   b) You roll a die (a cube with numbers from one to six on its faces)? _____

   c) A hockey team plays a championship match? _____

2. How many different outcomes are there when you:

   a) roll a die? _____   b) flip a coin? _____   c) play chess with a friend? _____

3. What are the possible outcomes for these spinners? The first one is done for you:

   a)   b)   c)   d)

   You spin a 1, 2, _____   _____   _____

   3 or 4   _____   _____   _____

   4   outcomes   _____ outcomes   _____ outcomes   _____ outcomes

4. You draw a marble from a box.
   How many different outcomes are there in
   each of the following cases?

   a) 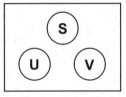   b)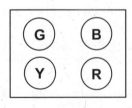

   _____ outcomes   _____ outcomes

5. List all the outcomes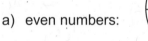
   that are…

   a) even numbers: _____

   b) odd numbers: _____

   c) greater than 9: _____

 jump math
MULTIPLYING POTENTIAL.

Probability & Data Management 2

PDM8-24: Counting Combinations

Abdul wants to know how many outcomes there are for a game with <u>two</u> spinners:

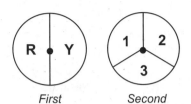

First spinner *Second spinner*

Step 1: There are 3 outcomes on the second spinner, so Abdul lists each colour on the first spinner 3 times.

First spinner	Second spinner
R	
R	
R	
Y	
Y	
Y	

Step 2: Beside each colour, Abdul writes the 3 possible outcomes on the second spinner.

First spinner	Second spinner
R	1
R	2
R	3
Y	1
Y	2
Y	3

The list shows that, altogether, there are <u>6 outcomes</u> for the game.

For each question below, answer parts a) and b) first.

Then complete the list of combinations to show all the ways Abdul can spin a colour and a number:

1.

First spinner	Second spinner

a) How many outcomes are on the second spinner?

_____

b) How many times should Abdul write B (for blue) and R (for red) on his list?

_____

c) How many outcomes does this game have altogether?

_____

2.

First spinner	Second spinner

a) How many outcomes are on the second spinner?

_____

b) How many times should Abdul write Y (for yellow) and G (for green) on his list?

_____

c) How many outcomes does this game have altogether?

_____

3.

First spinner	Second spinner

a) How many outcomes are on the second spinner?

_____

b) How many times should Abdul write G (for green), B (for blue) and Y (for yellow) on his list?

_____

c) How many outcomes does this game have altogether?

_____

4.

First spinner	Second spinner

a) How many outcomes are on the second spinner?

_____

b) How many times should Abdul write G (for green), B (for blue) and Y (for yellow) on his list?

_____

c) How many outcomes does this game have altogether?

_____

5. If you flip a coin there are two outcomes –
    heads (H) and tails (T).

    List all the outcomes for flipping a coin
    and spinning the spinner:

Coin	Spinner

6. Peter has a quarter and a dime in
    his left pocket, and a dime and a nickel
    in his right pocket. He pulls <u>one</u> coin from
    each pocket.

    List all the combinations of coins that he
    could pull out of his pockets:

Right pocket	Left pocket	Value of the coins

7. Clare can choose the following activities
    at art camp:

    Morning: painting or music

    Afternoon: drama, pottery or dance

    She makes a chart so she can see all of
    her choices. She starts by writing each
    of her morning choices 3 times:

    a) Complete the chart to show all of
        Clare's choices.

    b) Why did Clare write each of her
        choices for the morning 3 times?

Morning	Afternoon
painting	
painting	
painting	
music	
music	
music	

Answer the remaining questions in your notebook.

8. Make a chart to show all the activities you could choose at a camp that offered the following choices:

    Morning: swimming or tennis   **Afternoon:** canoeing, baseball or hiking

9.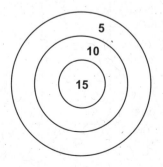

1st dart	2nd dart	Total Score

a) Record all scores you could
    get by throwing two darts at
    the dart board. (Assume both
    darts land on the board.)

b) Are there any combinations
    that give the same score?

jump math
MULTIPLYING POTENTIAL

Probability & Data Management 2

At sports camp, Erin can choose one of <u>two</u> sports in the morning (gymnastics or rowing) and one of <u>three</u> in the afternoon (volleyball, hockey, or rugby).

Erin draws a **tree diagram** so she can see all of her choices:

Step 1   She writes the name of her two morning choices at the end of two branches.

Step 2   Under each of her morning choices, she adds three branches (one for each of her three afternoon choices).

Step 3   Following any path along the branches (from the top of the tree to the bottom), you will find one of Erin's choices.

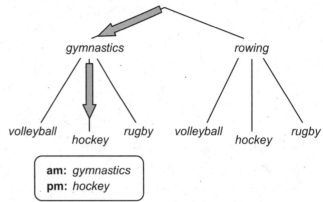

am: *gymnastics*
pm: *hockey*

Example: The path highlighted by arrows shows gymnastics in the morning and hockey in the afternoon.

----

1.   Follow a path from the top of the tree to a box at the bottom and write the sports named on the path in the box. Continue until you have filled in all the boxes:

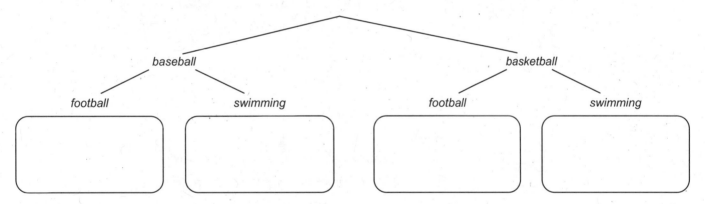

2.   Emma is playing a role playing game on a computer. Her character is exploring a tunnel in a cave.

List all the paths through the cave, using U for up and D for down:

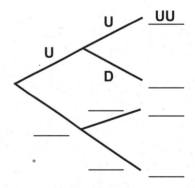

a)   How many paths are there through the cave? _____

b)   At the end of one path, a dragon is waiting.

Do you think it's likely or unlikely that Emma's character will meet the dragon? Explain:

_____

_____

3. Complete the tree diagram to show all of the possible outcomes from flipping a coin twice (H = heads and T = tails):

   NOTE: In a tree diagram you can write the outcomes on the branches (as in Question 2) or at the end of the branches.

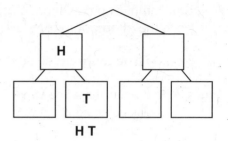

4. Complete the tree diagram to show all of the possible outcomes from first flipping a coin and then drawing a marble from the box:

 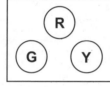 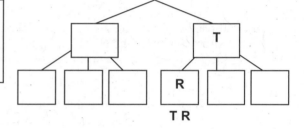

Answer the remaining questions in your notebook.

5. Matt's camp offers the following choices of activities: **Morning**: cricket or rowing

   Afternoon: tae kwon do or judo.

   In your notebook, draw a tree diagram (like the one in Question 1) to show all of his choices.

6. 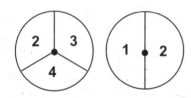 Draw a tree diagram to show all the combinations of numbers you could spin on the two spinners:

   a)   How many pairs of numbers add to four?

   b)   How many pairs of numbers have a product of four?

7. A restaurant offers the following choices for breakfast: **Main Course:** Eggs or Pancakes

   Juice: Apple, Orange or Grape

   Draw a tree diagram to show all the different breakfasts you could order.

8. Make a tree diagram to show all the combinations of points you could get throwing two darts.

   How many combinations add to 5?

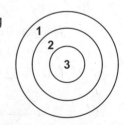

Fractions can be used to describe **probability**:

$\frac{3}{4}$ of the spinner is red, so the probability of spinning red is $\frac{3}{4}$.

There are 3 ways of spinning red and 4 ways of spinning *any* colour (either red or green).

The fraction $\frac{3}{4}$ compares the number of chances of spinning red (3, the numerator) to the number of chances of spinning *any* colour (4, the denominator).

----

1. For each of the following situations, how many ways are there of…

   a)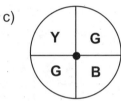

   … drawing a green marble?
   _____

   … drawing a marble of
   any colour?
   _____

   b)

   … drawing a red marble?
   _____

   … drawing a marble of
   any colour?
   _____

   c)

   … spinning green?
   _____

   … spinning any colour?
   _____

   d)

   … spinning green?
   _____

   … spinning any colour?
   _____

2. For each spinner, what's the probability (P)
   of spinning red?

   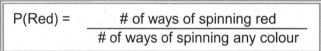

P(Red) =	# of ways of spinning red
	# of ways of spinning any colour

   a)

   P(Red) =

   b)

   P(Red) =

   c)

   P(Red) =

   d)

   P(Red) =

3. What is the probability of throwing a dart and hitting blue? Reduce your answer if possible:

   a)

B	R
G	B

   P(Blue) =

   b)

B	R	G

   P(Blue) =

   c)

B	R	R
G	B	Y

   P(Blue) =

   d)

R	B	G
Y		B

   P(Blue) =

4. For each spinner, write the probability of the given events:
   HINT: Cut the spinners into equal parts.

   a)

   P(Blue) =

   b)

   P(Red) =

   c)

   P(Yellow) =

   d)

   P(Green) =

5. Write a fraction for the probability of rolling a 1 on a die: _____

REMEMBER: A die has the numbers from 1 to 6 on its faces.

6. a) List the numbers on a die:

    _____

    b) How many outcomes are there when you roll a die?

    _____

7. a) List the numbers on a die that are even:

    _____

    b) How many ways can you roll an even number on a die?

    _____

    c) What is the probability of rolling an even number on a die?

    _____

8. a) List the numbers on a die that are greater than 4:

    _____

    b) How many ways can you roll a number greater than 4?

    _____

    c) What is the probability of rolling a number greater than 4 on a die?

    _____

9. Match the net for a cube (⬠) to the correct statement:

A 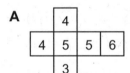   **B** 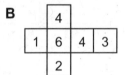   **C** 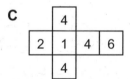   **D**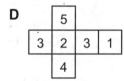

_____ The probability of rolling a 5 is $\frac{1}{6}$.   _____ The probability of rolling an even number is $\frac{1}{2}$.

_____ The probability of rolling a 4 is $\frac{1}{2}$.   _____ The probability of rolling a 1 is the same as the probability of rolling a 3.

Answer the following questions in your notebook.

10.   Write a fraction that gives the probability of spinning:

    a) the number 1.   b) the number 3.

    c) an even number.   d) an odd number.

    e) a number less than 5.   f) a number greater than 5.

11.   Write a fraction that gives the probability of spinning:

    a) the letter A.   b) the letter C.

    c) the letter E.   d) a vowel.

    e) a consonant.   f) a letter that appears in the word "Canada."

12. Clare says the probability of rolling a 5 on a die is $\frac{5}{6}$. Emma says the probability is $\frac{1}{6}$. Who is right? Explain.

13. Design a spinner on which the probability of spinning red is $\frac{3}{8}$.

NOTE: When two or more events have the same chance of occurring, the events are <u>equally likely</u>.

1. a) Are your chances of spinning red and yellow equally likely? Explain:

b) Are your chances of spinning red and yellow equally likely? Explain:

2. A game of chance is **fair** if both players have the same chance of winning.

Which of the following games are fair? For the games that aren't fair, which player has the better chance of winning?

a)

Player 1 must spin red to win.

Player 2 must spin blue to win.

Is it fair?   Y   N

b)

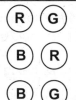

Player 1 must draw red to win.

Player 2 must draw blue to win.

Is it fair?   Y   N

3. Imogen throws a dart at the board.
Write the probability of the dart landing on each colour:

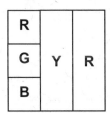

P(R) = _____

P(G) = _____

P(Y) = _____

P(B) = _____

4. Write letters A, B, and C on the spinner so that the probability of spinning:

➤ an A is .3

➤ a B is .5

➤ a C is .2

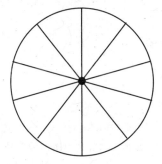

Answer the question below in your notebook.

5. The chart shows the ages of the boys and girls in Roger's class:

a) How many children are in the class?

b) A child is picked to make the morning announcement.
What is the probability the child is a girl?

c) What is the probability the child is a 9-year-old boy?

d) Make up your own problem using the numbers in the chart.

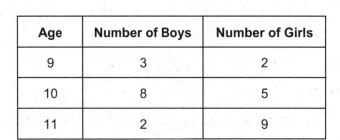

Age	Number of Boys	Number of Girls
9	3	2
10	8	5
11	2	9

1. Write a set of ordered pairs to show all the combinations you could spin on the two spinners:
   NOTE: The first one has been done for you, and the next two have been partially done.

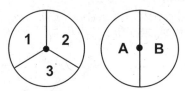

(_1_ , _A_)   (___ , _A_)   (___ , _A_)

(___ , ___)   (___ , ___)   (___ , ___)

a) How many outcomes are there? _____

b) How many ways can you spin...   (i)   a 1 on the first spinner and an A on the second? _____

(ii) an odd number on the first and a B on the second? _____

c) State the probability of spinning each situation in part b):   (i) _____   (ii) _____

2. a) In your notebook, write a set of ordered pairs to show
      all the combinations you could spin on these two spinners:

   b) State the probability of spinning...

      (i)   a 1 on the first spinner and an A on the second.

      (ii) an odd number on the first and a B on the second.

3. In your notebook, write a set of ordered pairs to show all the combinations for the following pairs:

   a) Flipping a coin and spinning a spinner:

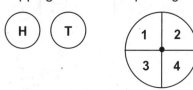

   b) Rolling a pair of tetrahedral dice:

4. Jason has a $5 bill and a $10 bill in his right pocket
   and a $5 bill and a $10 bill in his left pocket.

   He pulls one bill from each of his pockets:

   a) List the combinations of bills he could pull from
      his pockets.

   b) What is the probability that he will pull a pair of
      bills with a total value of $10?

Right pocket	Left pocket	Value of bills

Answer the following question in your notebook.

5. Cereal boxes come with either a picture of a cat or a dog inside. You win a prize if you
   collect one of each picture. Draw a tree diagram to find the probability that you will *not* win a
   prize if you buy...

   a) 2 boxes   b) 3 boxes   c) 4 boxes

Kate plans to spin the spinner 15 times to see how many times it will land on yellow.

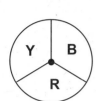

Since $\frac{1}{3}$ of the spinner is yellow, Kate **expects** to spin yellow $\frac{1}{3}$ of the time.

Kate finds $\frac{1}{3}$ of 15 by dividing by 3:   **15 ÷ 3 = 5**

So she expects the spinner to land on yellow <u>five</u> times.

NOTE: The spinner may not actually land on yellow five times, but five is the *most likely* number of "yellow" spins.

----

1. Shade <u>half</u> of the pie. How many pieces are in the whole pie? How many pieces are in half the pie?

   a)

   ____ pieces in half the pie

   ____ pieces in the pie

   b)

   ____ pieces in half the pie

   ____ pieces in the pie

   c)

   ____ pieces in half the pie

   ____ pieces in the pie

2. a) A pie is cut into four equal pieces. How many pieces make half? ____

   b) A pie is cut into eight equal pieces. How many pieces make half? ____

   c) A pie is cut into twelve equal pieces. How many pieces make half? ____

3. Write the number of pieces in the pie and the number of pieces shaded. Then circle the pies where <u>half</u> the pieces are shaded:

   a)

   ___ pieces shaded

   ___ pieces

   b)

   ___ pieces shaded

   ___ pieces

   c)

   ___ pieces shaded

   ___ pieces

   d)

   ___ pieces shaded

   ___ pieces

   e)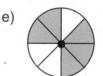

   ___ pieces shaded

   ___ pieces

4. Circle the pies where *half* the pieces are shaded. Put a large 'X' through the pies where *less than half* the pieces are shaded:

   HINT: Count the shaded and unshaded pieces first.

   a)   b)   c)   d)   e)   f)

Answer the remaining questions in your notebook.

5. Divide:

   a) $2\overline{)10}$ b) $2\overline{)12}$ c) $2\overline{)18}$ d) $2\overline{)26}$ e) $2\overline{)68}$ f) $2\overline{)82}$

6. Using long division, find…

   a) $\frac{1}{2}$ of 10   b) $\frac{1}{2}$ of 18   c) $\frac{1}{2}$ of 38   d) $\frac{1}{2}$ of 56

7. 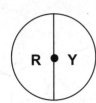 What fraction of your spins would you expect to be red?

   a) I would expect _____ of the spins to be red.

   b) If you spun the spinner 20 times, how many times would you expect to spin red? _____

8. If you flip a coin repeatedly, what fraction of the throws would you expect to be heads? _____

9. If you flip a coin 12 times, how many times would you expect to flip heads? Explain:

10. If you flipped a coin 40 times, how many times would you expect to flip heads?

11. If you flipped a coin 60 times, how many times would you expect to flip tails?

12. In your notebook find…

   $3\overline{)9}$ $3\overline{)21}$ $3\overline{)27}$ $3\overline{)33}$ $3\overline{)51}$ $3\overline{)63}$

   $4\overline{)12}$ $4\overline{)28}$ $4\overline{)36}$ $4\overline{)44}$ $4\overline{)64}$ $4\overline{)96}$

13. Fill in the missing numbers:

   a) $\frac{1}{3}$ of 12 is _____   b) $\frac{1}{3}$ of 18 is _____   c) $\frac{1}{3}$ of 21 is _____   d) $\frac{1}{3}$ of 30 is _____

   e) $\frac{1}{3}$ of 39 is _____   f) $\frac{1}{3}$ of 42 is _____   g) $\frac{1}{3}$ of 75 is _____   h) $\frac{1}{4}$ of 16 is _____

   i) $\frac{1}{4}$ of 32 is _____   j) $\frac{1}{4}$ of 48 is _____   k) $\frac{1}{4}$ of 56 is _____   l) $\frac{1}{4}$ of 76 is _____

14. For each spinner below, what *fraction* of your spins would you expect to be red?

   a) 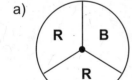 I would expect _____ of the spins to be red.

   b) 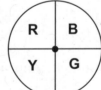 _____

   _____

15. How many times would you expect to spin *yellow* if you spun the spinner…

   a) 18 times?   b) 33 times?   c) 69 times?

   _____   _____   _____

   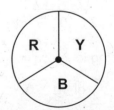

16.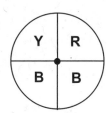

How many times would you expect to spin *red* if you spun the spinner…

a)   24 times?   b)   44 times?   c)   92 times?

_____   _____   _____

17.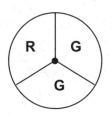

If you spun the spinner 15 times, how many times would you expect to spin *green*?

18. Colour the marbles red and green (or label them using R and G) to match the probability of drawing a marble of the given colour:

a) $P(Red) = \frac{1}{2}$ b) $P(Green) = \frac{1}{3}$ c) $P(Red) = \frac{3}{5}$

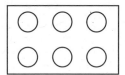   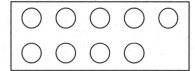   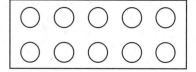

d) $P(Red) = \frac{3}{4}$ e) $P(Green) = \frac{2}{3}$ f) $P(Red) = \frac{1}{4}$

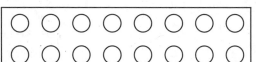   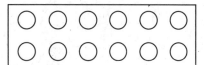   

Answer the remaining questions in your notebook.

19. Sketch a spinner on which you would expect to spin red $\frac{3}{4}$ of the time.

20. On a spinner, the probability of spinning yellow is $\frac{3}{4}$.

What is the probability of spinning a colour that is *not* yellow? Explain your answer with a picture.

21. How many times would you expect to spin blue if you used the spinner 50 times?

Explain your thinking.

22. How many times would you expect to spin yellow if you used the spinner 100 times?

Explain your thinking.

Probability & Data Management 2

PDM8-30: Describing Probability

- If an event cannot happen it is **impossible**.
  Example: Rolling the number 8 on a die is *impossible* (since a die only has the numbers 1, 2, 3, 4, 5, and 6 on its faces).

- If an event *must* happen it is **certain**.
  Example: When you roll a die it is *certain* that you will roll a number less than 7.

- It is **likely** that you would spin yellow on the spinner shown (since more than half the area of the spinner is yellow).

- It is **unlikely** that you would spin red on the spinner shown (since there is only a small section of the spinner that is red).

- When an event is expected to occur exactly half the time, we say that there is an **even** chance of the event occurring.

- -

1. Complete each statement by writing "more than half", "half" or "less than half":
   HINT: Start by finding half of the number by skip counting by 2s.

   a) 4 is _____ of 6   b) 3 is _____ of 9

   c) 6 is _____ of 10   d) 4 is _____ of 8

   e) 5 is _____ of 11   f) 7 is _____ of 15

   g) 7 is _____ of 12   h) 9 is _____ of 17

2. What fraction of your spins would you expect to be red: "half", "more than half", or "less than half"?

   a)   b)   c)   d)

   _____   _____   _____   _____

3. Describe each event as "likely", "unlikely" or "even":
   HINT: Start by finding out if the event will happen more than half the time or less than half the time.

   a)   b)   c)    d)

   spinning red is: spinning red is: spinning green is: spinning green is:

   _____   _____   _____   _____

4. Write **L** for Likely, **U** for Unlikely, or **E** for Even, beside each event:

   a) 16 marbles in a box; 4 red marbles   b) 18 marbles in a box; 9 red marbles
      <u>Event</u>: You draw a red marble. _____   <u>Event</u>: You draw a red marble. _____

   c) 9 socks in a drawer; 5 black socks   d) 21 pennies in a pocket; 10 Canadian
      <u>Event</u>: You pull out a black sock. _____   pennies.
                                                  <u>Event</u>: You pull out a Canadian penny. ____

 jump math
MULTIPLYING POTENTIAL

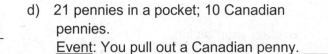 Probability & Data Management 2

5. Describe each event as "impossible", "unlikely", "likely" or "certain":

a)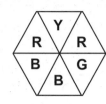

spinning blue is:

_____

b)

spinning red is:

_____

c)

spinning yellow is:

_____

d)

spinning yellow is:

_____

 6. Count the number of marbles of each colour.

Then fill in each blank with one of the following phrases: "less likely than," "more likely than" or "as likely as."

a) Drawing a red marble is _____ drawing a green.

b) Drawing a red marble is _____ drawing a yellow.

c) Drawing a blue marble is _____ drawing a green.

d) Drawing a white marble is _____ drawing a blue.

e) Drawing a red marble is _____ drawing a white.

7. Mark an 'X' on the number line to show the probability of spinning each colour:
   NOTE: Label each 'X' with the letter of the colour.

   ➢ red (R)   ➢ green (G)   ➢ yellow (Y)   ➢ blue (B)

0   1

8.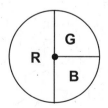

Which colour are you most likely to spin? _____

Which two colours are you least likely to spin? _____

Which word best describes your chances of spinning red?   Unlikely   Even   Likely

Which word best describes your chances of spinning green?   Unlikely   Even   Likely

9. Is each outcome on the spinner equally likely? Explain:

1. If you roll a die repeatedly, what fraction of the time would you expect to roll a 6? Explain:

2.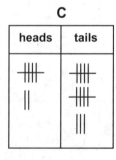

    Tanya and Daniel play a game of chance with the spinner shown.
    ➤ If it lands on yellow, Tanya wins.
    ➤ If it lands on red, Daniel wins.

    a) Tanya and Daniel play the game 20 times.
        How many times would you __predict__ that the spinner would land on red? _____

    b) When Tanya and Daniel play the game, they get the results
        shown in the chart:

        Daniel says the game isn't fair. Is he right? Explain.

        _____

        _____

        _____

        _____

Green	Red	Yellow
✚✚✚✚✚ ✚	✚✚✚✚	✚✚✚✚✚ ✚✚✚✚✚

3. If you flip a coin 20 times…

    a) How many of your flips
        would you expect to be heads? ____

    b) Which chart shows the
        result you would _most likely_ get? ____

    A

heads	tails
✚✚✚✚✚ ✚✚✚✚✚ ✚✚✚✚✚	✚✚✚✚✚

    B

heads	tails
✚✚✚✚✚ ✚✚✚✚✚ ✚	✚✚✚✚✚ ✚✚✚✚

    C

heads	tails
✚✚✚✚✚ ✚✚	✚✚✚✚✚ ✚✚✚✚✚ ✚✚✚

4. If you spun the spinner 18 times…

    a) How many of your spins
        would you expect to be
        green? ____

    b) Which of the charts shows
        a result you'd be most likely
        to get? ____

    c) Which result would surprise you? ____

    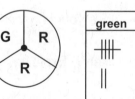

    A

green	red
✚✚✚✚✚ ✚✚	✚✚✚✚✚ ✚✚✚✚✚ ✚

    B

green	red
✚✚✚✚✚ ✚✚✚✚✚	✚✚✚✚✚ ✚✚✚

    C

green	red
✚✚✚✚✚ ✚✚✚✚✚ ✚✚✚✚✚ ✚✚	✚

Show your work for the following problems in your notebook.

1. Place the point of your pencil inside a paper clip in the middle of the spinner. Be sure to hold the pencil still so you can spin the paper clip around the pencil:

   a) If you spin the spinner 30 times, how many times would you predict spinning red? Show your work.
   HINT: Think of dividing 30 spins into three equal parts.

   b) Spin the spinner 30 times. Make a tally of your results. Did your results match your expectations?

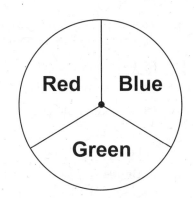

2.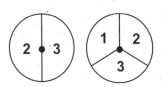

   a) Make a T-table and list all the outcomes for spinning the two spinners.

   b) Circle all the outcomes that add to 4.

   c) What is the probability of spinning a pair of numbers that add to 4?

   d) If you spin the spinner twelve times, how many times would you expect to spin a pair of numbers that add to 4?

3. You have 3 bills in your pocket – a $5 bill, a $10 bill, and a $50 bill. You reach in and pull out a <u>pair</u> of bills:

   a) What are all the possible combinations of two bills you could pull out?

   b) Could you expect to pull a pair of bills that add up to $15? Are the chances likely or unlikely?

   c) How did you solve the problem in part b)? Did you use a list? A picture? A calculation?

4. Write numbers on the spinners to match the probabilities given:

   a)
   The probability of spinning a 3 is $\frac{1}{4}$.

   b)
   The probability of spinning an even number is $\frac{5}{6}$.

   c)
   The probability of spinning a multiple of 3 is $\frac{2}{5}$.

   d)
   The probability of spinning a 2 is $\frac{1}{2}$.

5. Which outcome is more likely: A or B?

   A: You roll 2 dice and get a total of 12.   **B:** You toss a coin 3 times and get 3 heads.

6. The chart shows the record of a soccer team in its first ten games:

   If the team continues to play as well as they have been, how many of the next 30 games would you expect them to win?

Games Won	Games Lost	Games Tied
8	1	1

 jump math
MULTIPLYING POTENTIAL.

Probability & Data Management 2

Answer the questions below in your notebook.

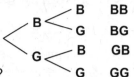

1. The tree diagram shows the possible combinations of boys (B) and
   girls (G) in a family of two children:
   a) What is the probability that a family with two children will have two boys?
   b) Draw a tree diagram for a family of three children.
   c) What is the probability that a family with three children will have two girls?

2.

Quarters	3	2	...
Dimes	0	1	...
Nickels	0	0	...
Value	$0.75	$0.60	...

Sandra has three coins, each less than 50¢.
None of the coins are pennies.
   a) Complete the chart to show all the combinations
      of coins that Sandra might have.
   b) What is the probability that the total value of
      Sandra's coins is $0.30?

3. Kyle has four coins, each worth less than 50¢.
   What is the probability that the total value of his coins is $.40?

4. Simone made an organized list to find all possible outcomes for rolling
   two dice. The table shows *part* of the chart she made:

   Why did Simone write the number 1 six times in her chart?
   Complete Simone's chart.

First Die	Second Die
1	1
1	2
1	3
1	4
1	5
1	6
2	1
2	2
2	3
2	4
2	5
2	6

5. When you roll two dice...
   HINT: Answer the questions below using the chart you made in Question 4.
   a) What is the probability of rolling a total of:

      i) 4   ii) 6   iii) 7   iv) 11   v) 12

   b) What is the probability of rolling:

      i) an even number   ii) two matching numbers   iii) two consecutive numbers

   c) What are the two least likely totals you can roll?   d) What total are you *most* likely to roll?

6. a) A true and false test has two questions. Make an organized list and a tree diagram to find the
      probability that *both* of the questions are true.

   BONUS:
   b) A true and false test has two questions. Eschi made an organized list to find all possible truth
      values for the three questions:

First question	T	T	T	T	F	F	F	F
Second question								
Third question								

      i) Why did she write T four times in the row for the first question?
      ii) Complete Eschi's chart.

Answer the following questions in your notebook.

1. The probability of rain is often given as a percent. For each prediction below, write a fraction giving the probability that it will *not* rain:
   NOTE: Reduce your answer to lowest terms.

   a) 60% chance of rain   b) 35% chance of rain   c) 75% chance of rain

2. **Batting averages** are decimals that can be changed to fractions out of 1000.

   > *Example:*   A batting average of .427 ($= \frac{427}{1000}$) means:
   >
   > "Out of 1000 times at bat, the player has scored 427 hits."

   Change the following batting averages to fractions:
   NOTE: Reduce your answers to lowest terms.

   a) .125   b) .300   c) .425   d) .256   e) .324

3. Say how many hits, on average, each player is likely to get in 60 times at bat:
   HINT: First reduce each average to lowest terms.

   a) Player A's   b) Player B's   c) Player C's
      batting average: .200   batting average: .250   batting average: .400

4. In each case say which player is more likely to have a hit:

   a) Player A: batting average .425   b) Player A: hits one quarter of pitches
      Player B: hits 4 out of 10 pitches   Player B: batting average .230
      Player C: hits 42% of pitches   Player C: hits 23% of pitches

5. The pie diagram shows the fraction of students at a school who walk, bus, bike or skateboard to school:

   If you surveyed 200 students about how many would you expect to have skateboarded to school?

   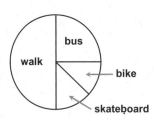

6. A lake contains approximately 1000 fish. A scientist observes 50 fish and finds that 7 are trout. How many trout are likely to be in the lake?

7. In the game of MONOPOLY you get an extra turn if you roll matching numbers on a pair of dice (i.e. 2 ones, 2 twos, etc.).
   What is the probability of getting an extra turn in MONOPOLY?

G8-18: Complementary Angles

Complementary angles are angles whose sum is 90°.

Example:

 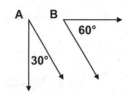

Complementary angles: **∠1 and ∠2**   **∠A and ∠B**

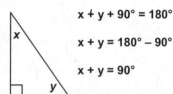

NOTE:
The two non-right angles in a right triangle are complementary angles:

$x + y + 90° = 180°$

$x + y = 180° - 90°$

$x + y = 90°$

---

1.   Find the complementary angles:

a)

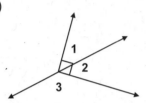

_____ and _____

b)

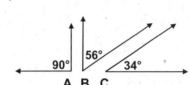

_____ and _____

c)

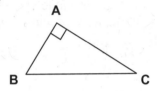

_____ and _____

d)

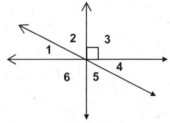

_____ and _____

_____ and _____

e)

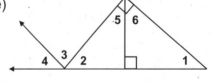

∠2 and ____, ∠2 and ____

∠6 and ____, ∠6 and ____

f)

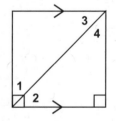

∠1 and ____, ∠1 and ____

∠4 and ____, ∠4 and ____

2.   Find the value of x:

a)

∠x = _____

b)

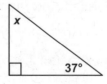

∠x = _____

c)

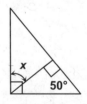

∠x = _____

G8-19: Supplementary Angles

Supplementary angles are angles whose sum is 180°.

Examples:

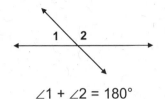   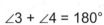   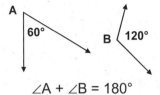

∠1 + ∠2 = 180°   ∠3 + ∠4 = 180°   ∠A + ∠B = 180°

---

1. Find the supplementary angles in each graph below:

a)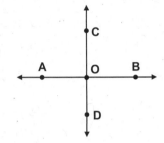

b)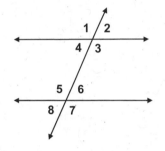

c)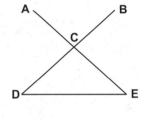

∠AOC + _____ = 180°   ∠2 + ___ = 180°, ∠6 + ___ = 180°   ∠ACD + _____ = 180°

∠AOC + _____ = 180°   ∠2 + ___ = 180°, ∠6 + ___ = 180°   _____ + _____ = 180°

∠AOD + _____ = 180°   ∠4 + ___ = 180°, ∠8 + ___ = 180°   _____ + _____ = 180°

∠BOD + _____ = 180°   ∠4 + ___ = 180°, ∠8 + ___ = 180°   _____ + _____ = 180°

Given the following diagram, find ∠x:

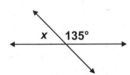

Solution:
∠x + 135° = 180° (Supplementary angles)
∠x = 180° − 135°
∠x = 45°

---

2. Find ∠x and ∠y, or ∠x + ∠y:

a)

b)

c)

d)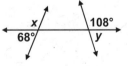

∠x = _____   ∠x = _____   ∠x = _____   ∠x = _____, ∠y = _____

e)

f)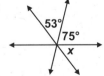

g)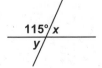

h)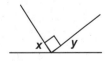

∠x = ___, ∠y = ____   ∠x = _____   ∠x = ___, ∠y = ____   ∠x + ∠y = _____

MULTIPLYING POTENTIAL.

Geometry 2

G8-20: Opposite Angles

Opposite angles are non-adjacent angles formed by intersecting lines:

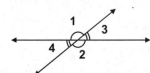

∠1 and ∠2 are opposite angles

∠3 and ∠4 are also opposite angles

∠1 + ∠3 = 180°, so ∠1 = 180° − ∠3
∠2 + ∠3 = 180°, so ∠2 = 180° − ∠3
so ∠1 ≅ ∠2

Opposite angles are **congruent** (written as: ∠1 ≅ ∠2 and ∠3 ≅ ∠4).

NOTE: There are no opposite angles in the figures below because there are no intersecting lines.

One exception:

1. Find angles that are opposite (and congruent):

a)

∠AOC ≅ _____

∠AOD ≅ _____

b)
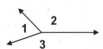

_____ ≅ _____

_____ ≅ _____

c)
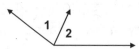

∠1 ≅ _____, ∠2 ≅ _____

∠5 ≅ _____, ∠6 ≅ _____

d)
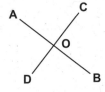

_____ ≅ _____, _____ ≅ _____

_____ ≅ _____

e)
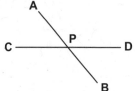

_____ ≅ _____

_____ ≅ _____

f)
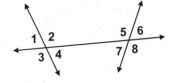

_____ ≅ _____

_____ ≅ _____

2. Find the missing angles:

a)
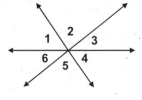

∠x = _____

b)

∠x = _____, ∠y = _____

c)
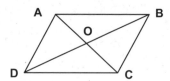

∠x = _____, ∠y = _____, ∠z = _____

d)
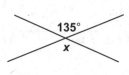

∠x = _____, ∠y = _____

e)
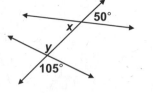

∠x = _____, ∠y = _____

f)
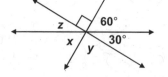

∠x = _____, ∠y = _____, ∠z = _____

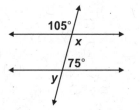

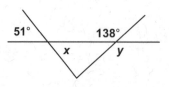

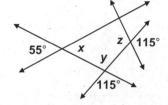

G8-21: Transversals and Corresponding Angles

A **transversal** is a line that crosses two or more lines:

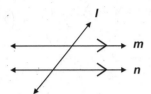 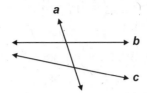 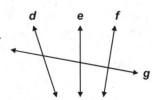

Lines *l*, *a* and *g* are transversals.

----

1. Identify the transversals in the pictures below:

a)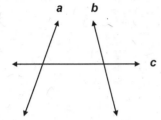

Transversal: _____

b)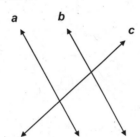

Transversal: _____

c)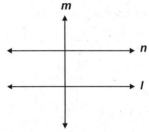

Transversal: _____

d)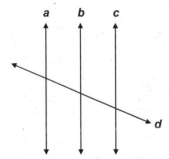

Transversal: _____

e)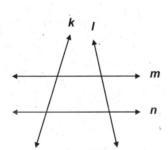

Transversals: _____

f)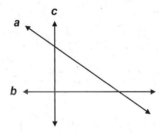

Transversals: _____

2. Draw a transversal that intersects line *a* at 90°.

   At what angle does the transversal intersect line *b*? _____

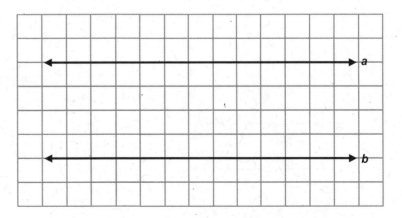

3. Repeat Question 2 with a transversal that intersects line *a* at 45°.

G8-22: Transversals and Corresponding Angles (Advanced)

Angles that are on the same side of a transversal (and on the same side of the two lines crossed by the transversal) are called **corresponding angles**.

Corresponding angles are congruent when the lines crossed by the transversal are parallel.

Example:

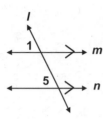 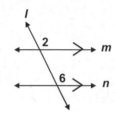 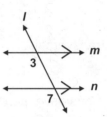 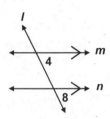

Corresponding angles: ∠1 ≅ ∠5   ∠2 ≅ ∠6   ∠3 ≅ ∠7   ∠4 ≅ ∠8

- -

1. List the corresponding angles that are <u>congruent</u>:

   a)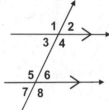

   b)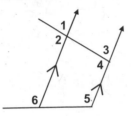

   c)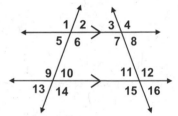

   a) ∠1 and _____, ∠3 and _____

   ∠2 and _____, ∠4 and _____

   b) ∠1 and _____, ∠2 and _____

   ∠5 and _____

   c) ∠3 and _____, ∠5 and _____

   ∠7 and _____, ∠10 and _____

2. Find the measure of the corresponding angles:

   a)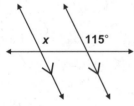

   b)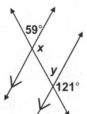

   c)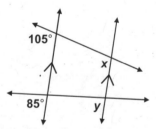

   ∠x = _____

   ∠x = _____, ∠y = _____

   ∠x = _____, ∠y = _____

   d)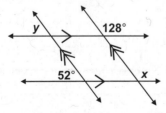

   e)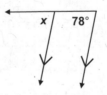

   f)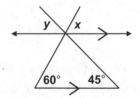

   ∠x = _____, ∠y = _____

   ∠x = _____

   ∠x = _____, ∠y = _____

G8-23: Alternate Angles

Alternate angles are found on opposite sides of a transversal (and between the lines crossed by the transversal).

Alternate angles are <u>congruent</u> when the lines a transversal crosses are parallel:

Example:

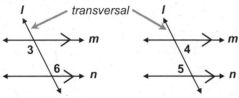

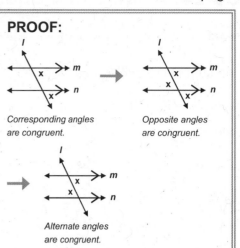

PROOF:

Corresponding angles are congruent.

Opposite angles are congruent.

Alternate angles are congruent.

Alternate angles: ∠3 ≅ ∠6   ∠4 ≅ ∠5

---

1. Find the alternate angle that is congruent to the given angle:

a)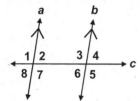

b)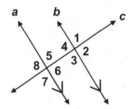

c)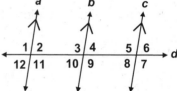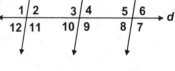

∠2 and _____

∠3 and _____

∠4 and _____

∠11 and _____, ∠4 and _____

∠10 and _____, ∠5 and _____

2. Find the missing angles:

a)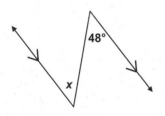

b)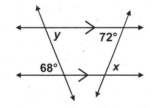

c)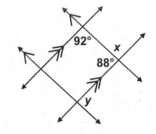

∠x = _____

∠x = _____, ∠y = _____

∠x = _____, ∠y = _____

3. Fill in *all* the missing angles using what you know about opposite, supplementary, corresponding and alternate angles:

a)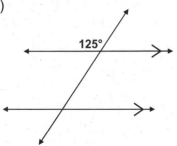

b)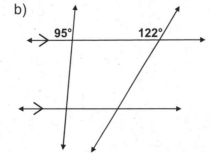

c)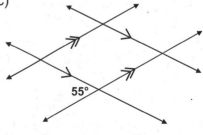

TEACHER: Activity 2 in the Teacher's Guide (listed for this section) is better done with G8–28: Interior Angles in a Polygon.

The sum of the angles in a triangle is 180°.

Example:

Find ∠x:

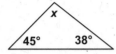

Solution: x + 45° + 38° = 180°
x = 180° − 45° − 38°
x = 97°

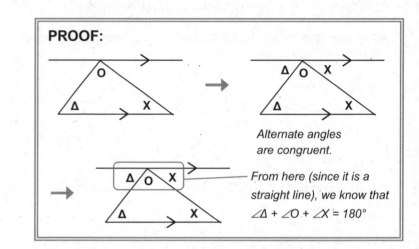

PROOF:

Alternate angles are congruent.

From here (since it is a straight line), we know that
∠Δ + ∠O + ∠X = 180°

---

1.   Find the missing angles. Show your work in your notebook:

a)

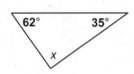

∠x = _____

b)

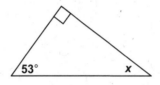

∠x = _____

c)

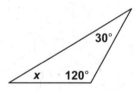

∠x = _____

d)

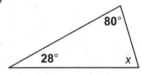

∠x = _____

e)

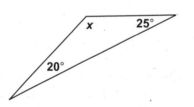

∠x = _____

f)

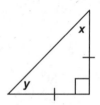

∠x = _____, ∠y = _____

g)

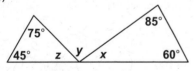

∠x = _____

∠y = _____

∠z = _____

h)

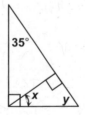

∠x = _____

∠y = _____

i)

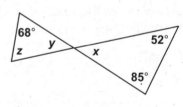

∠x = _____

∠y = _____

∠z = _____

G8-25: Exterior Angles

An **exterior angle** is formed by extending a side of a triangle. Angle x is an exterior angle:

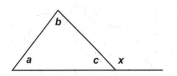

An **exterior angle** is equal to the sum of the two opposite interior angles ($x = a + b$).

Example 1:

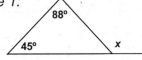

$x = 88° + 45°$
$\quad = 133°$

Example 2:

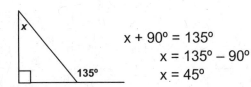

$x + 90° = 135°$
$x = 135° - 90°$
$x = 45°$

PROOF:
$\qquad a + b + c = 180°$ (SATT)
$\qquad\qquad x + c = 180°$ (SAT)
So $\qquad a + b + c = x + c$
But then $\qquad a + b = x$

---

1. Find the missing angles. Show your work in your notebook:

a)

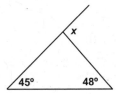

$\angle x =$ _____

b)

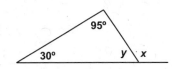

$\angle x =$ _____, $\angle y =$ _____

c)

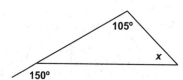

$\angle x =$ _____

d)

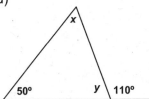

$\angle x =$ _____, $\angle y =$ _____

e)

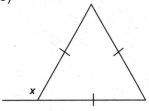

$\angle x =$ _____

f)

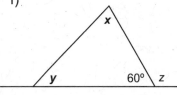

$\angle x + \angle y =$ ___, $\angle z =$ ___

g)

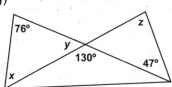

$\angle x =$ ___, $\angle y =$ ___, $\angle z =$ ___

h)

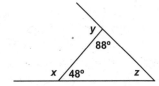

$\angle x =$ ___, $\angle y =$ ___, $\angle z =$ ___

i)

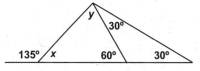

$\angle x =$ _____, $\angle y =$ _____

jump math
MULTIPLYING POTENTIAL

Geometry 2

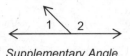

Supplementary Angle
Theorem (SAT)
$\angle 1 + \angle 2 = 180º$

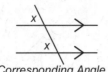

Corresponding Angle
Theorem (CAT)

Alternate Angle
Theorem (AAT)

Opposite Angle
Theorem (OAT)

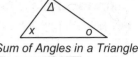

Sum of Angles in a Triangle
Theorem (SATT)
$x + o + \Delta = 180º$

----

1. Find the missing angles. List the Theorem you used to find each angle. The first question is done for you:

    HINT: Fill in as many missing angles as you can. Use the theorems above.

a)

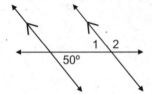

$\angle 1 =$ <u>50°</u> (AAT)

$\angle 2 =$ <u>130°</u> (SAT)

b)

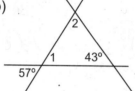

$\angle 1 =$ _____ ( )

$\angle 2 =$ _____ ( )

c)

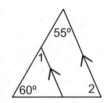

$\angle 1 =$ _____ ( )

$\angle 2 =$ _____ ( )

d)

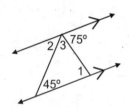

$\angle 1 =$ _____ ( )

$\angle 2 =$ _____ ( )

$\angle 3 =$ _____ ( )

e)

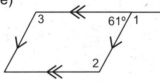

$\angle 1 =$ _____ ( )

$\angle 2 =$ _____ ( )

$\angle 3 =$ _____ ( )

f)

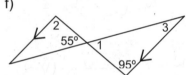

$\angle 1 =$ _____ ( )

$\angle 2 =$ _____ ( )

$\angle 3 =$ _____ ( )

g)

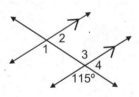

$\angle 1 =$ _____ ( )

$\angle 2 =$ _____ ( )

$\angle 3 =$ _____ ( )

$\angle 4 =$ _____ ( )

h)

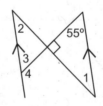

$\angle 1 =$ _____ ( )

$\angle 2 =$ _____ ( )

$\angle 3 =$ _____ ( )

$\angle 4 =$ _____ ( )

i)

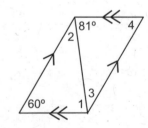

$\angle 1 =$ _____ ( )

$\angle 2 =$ _____ ( )

$\angle 3 =$ _____ ( )

$\angle 4 =$ _____ ( )

G8-26: Problem Solving Using Angle Properties *(continued)* page 283

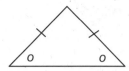

Isosceles Triangle Theorem (ITT)

The **base angles** in an isosceles triangle are **equal**.

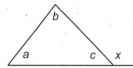

Exterior Angle Theorem (EAT)

An **exterior angle** is equal to the sum of the **two opposite interior angles**, x = a + b.

2. To find the missing angles you will need to find some angles that aren't marked. Write a number for each angle you used on the diagram. Say what theorem you used to find each angle:

a)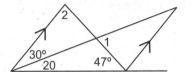

b)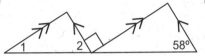

c)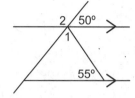

_____   _____   _____

_____   _____   _____

_____   _____   _____

_____   _____   _____

3. Follow the instructions for Question 2 to find the missing angles. Show your work in your notebook (you will need to use ITT and EAT):

a)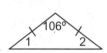

b)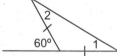

c)

d)

∠1 = ____   ∠1 = ____   ∠1 = ____   ∠1 = ____

∠2 = ____   ∠2 = ____   ∠2 = ____   ∠2 = ____

4. Recall that two triangles are similar if their corresponding angles are all equal. In your notebook say how you know each of the statements below is true:

   HINT: Number the angles and say what theorem you used to prove each pair of corresponding angles is equal.

a)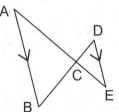

b)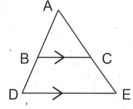

c)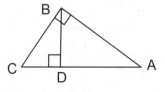

△ABC and △CDE are similar   △ABC and △ADE are similar   △ABC, △CDB and △ADB are similar

jump math
MULTIPLYING POTENTIAL

Geometry 2

G8-27: Finding Missing Angles

1. Use the Angle Theorems from section G8-26. Write an expression for each figure below (write the abbreviation for the Theorem you used beside your equation). Then solve the equation:

Example:

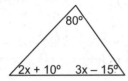

2x + 10° + 3x − 15° + 80° = 180° (SATT)
2x + 3x = 180° − 10° + 15° − 80°
5x = 105°
x = 21°

NOTE:

For some questions on this page you will need the
Isosceles Triangle Theorem (ITT)
and the Exterior Angle Theorem (EAT).

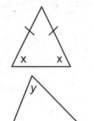

The base angles in an isosceles triangle are equal (ITT)

An exterior angle of a triangle is equal in magnitude to the sum of the two opposite interior angles (EAT)

Show your work for the following questions in your notebook.

a)

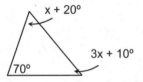

x = _____

b)

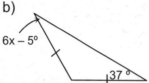

x = _____

c)

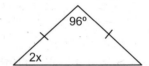

x = _____

d)

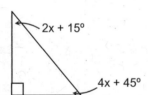

x = _____

e)

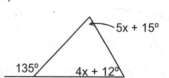

x = _____

f)

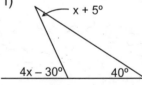

x = _____

g)

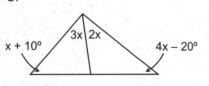

x = _____

h)

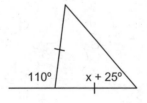

x = _____

i)

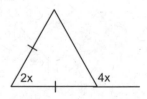

x = _____

Geometry 2

G8-28: Interior Angles in a Polygon

TEACHER: Activity 2 listed for G8-24 in the Teacher's Guide is better done with this worksheet.

A pentagon can be divided into three triangles. The sum of the interior angles in a triangle is 180°. So the sum of interior angles in a pentagon is 180° × 3 = 540°.

Example: Find the sum of all interior angles of a polygon:

Pentagon

Divide the pentagon into 3 triangles by drawing diagonals from one vertex.

1. Fill in the table below, find the sum of the interior angles of the polygons:

a)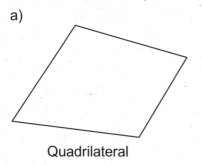
Quadrilateral

b)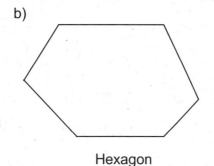
Hexagon

c)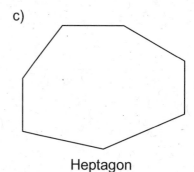
Heptagon

d)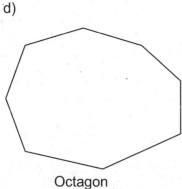
Octagon

e)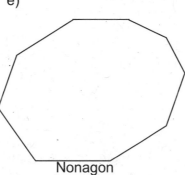
Nonagon

f)
Decagon

Polygons	Number of sides	Number of triangles created by diagonals	Expression for the sum of interior angles	Sum of interior angles
Quadrilateral				
Pentagon	5	3	180° × 3	540°
Hexagon				
Heptagon				
Octagon				
Nonagon				
Decagon				

2. What is the relationship between the number of sides and the sum of the interior angles of a polygon? Write an equation for this relationship in your notebook.

Geometry 2

G8-29: Concepts in Geometry (Triangles)

1.

   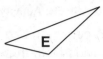

Without measuring the triangles, match each triangle with its description:

_____ isosceles, right-angled   _____ obtuse scalene   _____ equilateral

_____ obtuse isosceles   _____ scalene right-angled

2.   Measure each side length for each triangle and answer the following questions:

a)

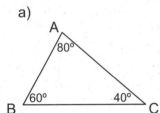

AB = _____mm

AC = _____mm

BC = _____mm

The longest side is opposite the _____° angle.

The shortest side is opposite the _____° angle.

b)

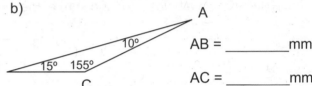

AB = _____mm

AC = _____mm

BC = _____mm

The longest side is opposite the _____° angle.

The shortest side is opposite the _____° angle.

c)

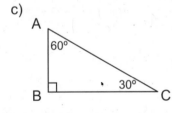

AB = _____mm

AC = _____mm

BC = _____mm

The longest side is opposite the _____° angle.

The shortest side is opposite the _____° angle.

d)

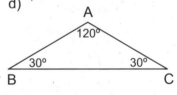

AB = _____mm

AC = _____mm

BC = _____mm

The longest side is opposite the _____° angle.

The shortest sides are opposite the _____° angles.

3.   Look at the length of the sides and the sizes of the angles opposite those sides in question 1. Write down a rule they seem to follow:

4.   In your notebook, either sketch an example or state that it does not exist:

   a)   an isosceles obtuse triangle   b)   an equilateral obtuse triangle
   c)   an equilateral right triangle   d)   a scalene right triangle
   e)   a scalene acute triangle   f)   an isosceles right triangle
   g)   an isosceles right triangle where the shortest side is unique.
      HINT: Can the two longest sides both be adjacent to a right angle?

jump math
MULTIPLYING POTENTIAL.

Geometry 2

1. On grid paper, using only a straight edge draw…
   a) an isosceles triangle with height 4 units
   b) a parallelogram with a 45° angle
   c) an obtuse scalene triangle
   e) a pentagon with two 135° angles
   d) a trapezoid with two right angles

2.

   On grid paper draw 9 dots in the position shown in Figure 1. Join sets of dots to make as many polygons as you can as shown in Figures 2 and 3.

   Figure 1   Figure 2   Figure 3

   a) How many non-congruent triangles can you make by joining the dots?
   b) How many non-congruent quadrilaterals can you make?
   c) Classify the quadrilaterals you make (i.e. as squares, rectangles, trapezoids, etc.)
   d) Classify the polygons you made by the number of sides (i.e. as triangles, quadrilaterals, etc.).
   e) Classify the polygons you made by the number of lines of symmetry that they have.

3. Show how many non-congruent shapes you can make by adding one square to the original figure:

   a)   b)   c)

4. A tetromino is a figure made of 4 squares: each square shares a complete edge with at least one other square. How many different tetrominoes can you make?

   Tetromino   Not Tetrominoes

5. What is the maximum number of lines of symmetry in a triangle?

6. A triangle has one line of symmetry and a perimeter of 12 cm.
   The shortest side of the triangle is 2 cm long. How long are the other sides?

7. In a 3 by 3 array, shade 4 squares so the resulting shape has…

   a) no lines of symmetry   b) one line of symmetry

   c) 4 lines of symmetry

8. A pentomino is like a tetromino, but is made of 5 squares.
   How many pentominoes can you find?
   How many lines of symmetry does each pentomino have?

Geometry 2

G8-31: Introduction to Coordinate Systems

The position of a point on a coordinate grid is identified by a pair of numbers in a bracket:

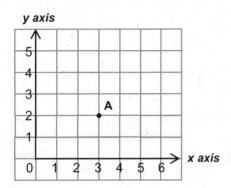

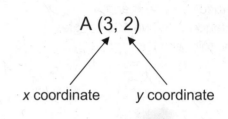

A (3, 2)

x coordinate   *y* coordinate

---

1. Fill in the coordinates for the given points:

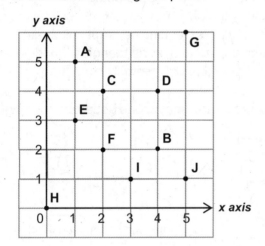

A (,   )   B (,   )

C (,   )   D (,   )

E (,   )   F (,   )

G (,   )   H (,   )

I (,   )   J (,   )

A grid that has been extended to include negative integers is called a **Cartesian coordinate system**:

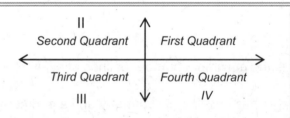

2. a) Identify and label the origin (0) and the x- and y-axes.

    b) Label the axes with positive and negative integers.

    c) Number the four quadrants (using I, II, III, IV).

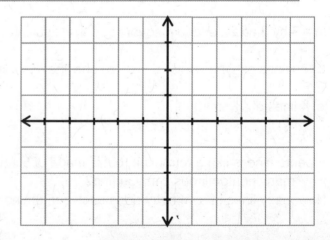

Geometry 2

G8-32: Plotting Points in Coordinate Systems

1. In Figure 1, point A (2, 3) is in the first quadrant.
    Its x- and y-coordinates are <u>both positive</u>.

    a)   Plot and label:

B (3, 2)	C (1, 5)
D (4, 1)	E (2, 6)

    b)   Find the coordinates of points:

    P (,   )   Q (,   )

    R (,   )   S (,   )

Figure 1:

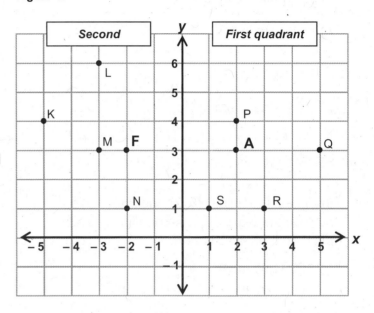

2. In Figure 1, point F (−2, 3) is in the second quadrant. Its x-coordinate is <u>negative</u> and its y-coordinate is <u>positive</u>.

    a)   Plot and label:

G (−3, 2)	H (−1, 5)
I (−4, 1)	J (−5, 3)

    b)   Find the coordinates of points:

    K (,   )   L (,   )

    M (,   )   N (,   )

3. In Figure 2, point A (−2, −3) is in the third quadrant. Its x- and y- coordinates are <u>both negative</u>.

    a)   Plot and label:

B (−3, −2)	C (−1, −5)
D (−4, −3)	E (−5, −2)

    b)   Find the coordinates of points:

    K (,   )   L (,   )

    M (,   )   N (,   )

Figure 2:

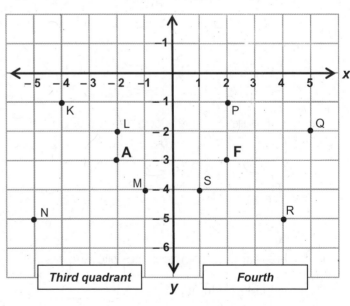

4. In Figure 2, point F (2, -3) is in the fourth quadrant. Its x-coordinate is <u>positive</u> and its y-coordinate is <u>negative</u>.

    a)   Plot and label:

G (3, −2)	H (1, −5)
I (4, −1)	J (5, −6)

    b)   Find the coordinates of points:

    P (,   )   Q (,   )

    R (,   )   S (,   )

5. In Figure 1, points B (2, 0) and C (−4, 0) are both on the x-axis. The y-coordinate of any point on the x-axis is <u>zero</u>.

    a) Plot and label:

        A (3, 0)   M (−3, 0)

        N (5, 0)   O (−1, 0)

    b) Find the coordinates of points:

        P (,   )   Q (,   )

        R (,   )   S (,   )

Figure 1

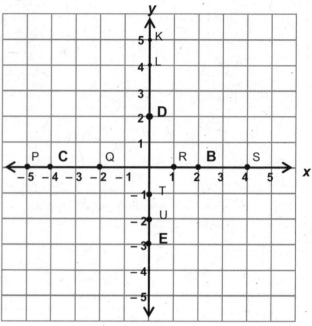

6. In Figure 1, points D (0, 2) and E (0, −3) are both on the y-axis. The x-coordinate of any point on the y-axis is <u>zero</u>.

    a) Plot and label:

        G (0, 1)   H (0, −4)

    b) Find the coordinates of points:

        K (,   )   L (,   )

        T (,   )   U (,   )

Figure 2

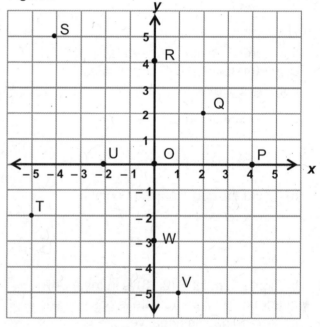

7. a) Locate and label the points on Figure 2:

        A (3, 4)   B (5, −2)

        C (−3, −2)   D (−4, 1)

        E (3, 0)   F (0, 2)

        G (0, 3)   H (−5, 0)

    b) On Figure 2, find the coordinates of points:

        P (,   )   Q (,   )

        R (,   )   S (,   )

        T (,   )   U (,   )

        V (,   )   W (,   )

    c) Use letters to complete the following blanks:

        First quadrant points - _____   Second quadrant points - _____

        Third quadrant points - _____   Fourth quadrant points - _____

        Points on x-axis - _____   Points on y-axis - _____

        Origin - _____

1. Add a point D so that the four points form the vertices of...

a) ... a <u>rectangle</u>:

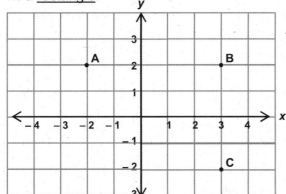

Then write the coordinates of the four vertices in the shape:

A (,   ) B (,   ) C (,   ) D (,   )

b) ... a <u>parallelogram</u>:

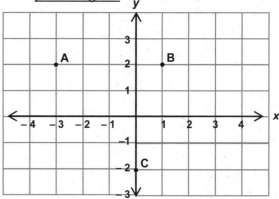

Then write the coordinates of the four vertices in the shape:

A (,   ) B (,   ) C (,   ) D (,   )

NOTE: There are two possible answers.

Answer the following questions on grid paper.

2. Plot each set of points on the Cartesian plane:

a) (2, −2) (2, −1) (2, 0) (2, 1) (2, 2)

b) (−3, −4) (−3, −2) (−3, 0) (−3, 2) (−3, 4)

c) (−10, 5) (−5, 5) (0, 5) (5, 5) (10, 5)

d) (−10, −4) (0, −4) (10, −4)

e) (−1, −2) (0, −1) (1, 0) (2, 1) (3, 2) (4, 3)

3. Draw a line that joins the points in each set of a), b), c), d) in Question 2 above. In each case tell which axis the line is parallel to.

4. What is the relationship between the x-coordinate and y-coordinate in each coordinate pair in part e) in Question 2? Join the points in e). What kind of figure have you created?

5. Plot and join the points in each group. Identify the polygon drawn:

a) A (−2, 2) B (3, 2) C (3, 5)

b) D (1, 1) E (1, -1) F (−1, 1) G (−1, −1)

c) H (−2, −3) I (2, −3) J (0, 4) K (−1, −2) L (1, −2)

6. Draw three Cartesian planes, design the following polygons and then write down the coordinates for each of the vertices:

a) A triangle that is in the first and second quadrants.

b) A square with each vertex in a different quadrant.

c) A right triangle with one leg on the x-axis and the other leg on the y-axis.

G8-34: Translations

1. How many units right or left and how many units up or down did the dot slide from position A to B?

a)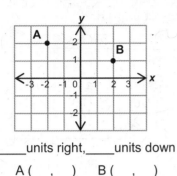

____units right,____units down

A (,) B (,)

b)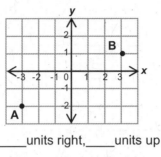

____units right,____units up

A (,) B (,)

c)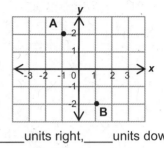

____units right,____units down

A (,) B (,)

2. Slide the point…

a) 5 units right; 2 units down

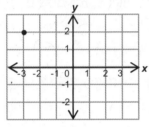

Original point (,)

image (,)

b) 6 units left; 3 units up

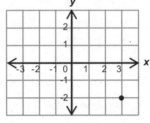

Original point (,)

image (,)

c) 3 units left; 4 units down

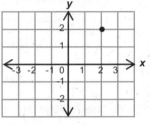

Original point (,)

image (,)

3. Slide the point two units down, then copy the shape, write down the coordinates of the point and its image:

a)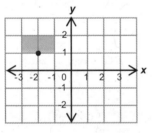

Original point (,)

image (,)

b)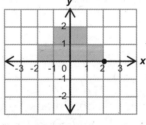

Original point (,)

image (,)

c)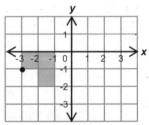

Original point (,)

image (,)

4. Slide each figure 5 units to the right and 3 units down:

a)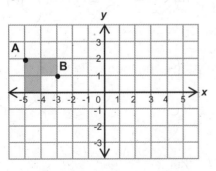

A (,) ⟶ A' (,); B (,) ⟶ B' (,)

b)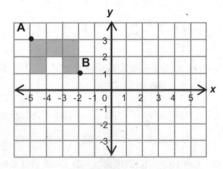

A (,) ⟶ A' (,); B (,) ⟶ B' (,)

5.

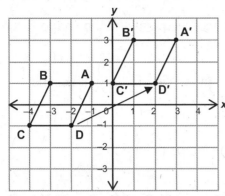

a) Describe how the point D moved to the point D′ :

_____

b) Draw an arrow to show where point A moved to under the translation.

c) Describe how point A moved:

_____

d) Did all of the points on the square move by the same amount? _____

e) A (,)⟼A′ (,); B (,)⟼B′ (,); C (,)⟼C′ (,); D (,)⟼D′ (,)

6. Draw a translation arrow from a vertex of shape A to the corresponding vertex in A′.
   Then describe how far the shape slid in moving from position A to A′.

a)

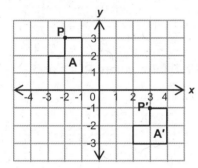

P (,)

↓

P′ (,)

b)

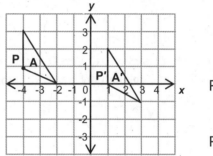

P (,)

↓

P′ (,)

7. Slide the shapes in the grids below. Describe how far the shape moved (right/left and up/down):

a)

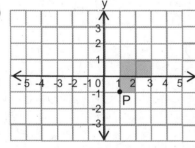

P (,)

↓

P′ (,)

b)

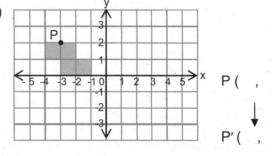

P (,)

↓

P′ (,)

My slide: _____

My slide: _____

Answer the following questions in your notebook.

8. Draw a shape on a four quadrant coordinate system. Translate the shape and draw a translation arrow between a point on the shape and a point on the image. Describe how far the shape moved (right/left and up/down).

9. Draw 2 four quadrant coordinate systems on grid paper. Draw the given shapes. Translate the shape and write the coordinates of its new vertices.

   a) Square with vertices A (1, 1), B (1, 3), C (3, 3), D (3, 1) Translate 3 units right, 4 up

   b) Triangle with vertices A (3, 7), B (2, 5), C (5, 4) Translate 4 units right, 3 down

G8-35: Reflections

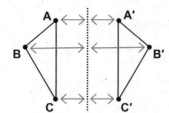

When a point is **reflected** in a mirror line, the point and the image of the point are the same distance from the mirror line.

A figure and its image are congruent but face in opposite directions.

---

1. Reflect the point P using the x-axis as the mirror line. Label the image point P′:

a)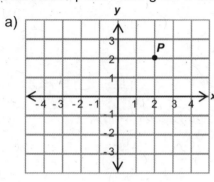

P (,) → P′ (,)

b)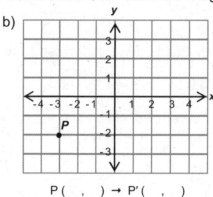

P (,) → P′ (,)

c)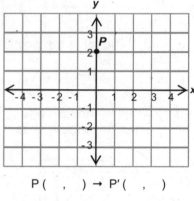

P (,) → P′ (,)

2. Reflect the set of points P, Q and R through the x-axis. Label the image points P′, Q′ and R′:

   HINT: The image of a point on the x-axis through the x-axis is the point itself.

a)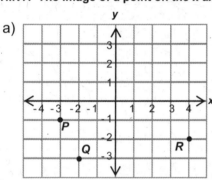

P (,) → P′ (,)
Q (,) → Q′ (,)
R (,) → R′ (,)

b)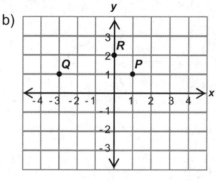

P (,) → P′ (,)
Q (,) → Q′ (,)
R (,) → R′ (,)

c)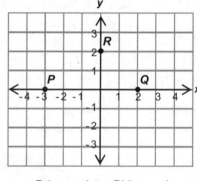

P (,) → P′ (,)
Q (,) → Q′ (,)
R (,) → R′ (,)

3. Reflect the figure by first reflecting the points on the figure through the x-axis:

a)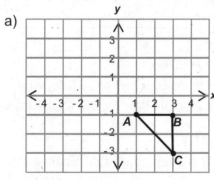

A (,) → A′ (,)
B (,) → B′ (,)
C (,) → C′ (;)

b)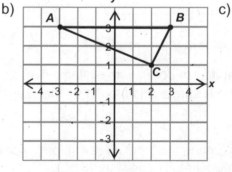

A (,) → A′ (,)
B (,) → B′ (,)
C (,) → C′ (,)

c)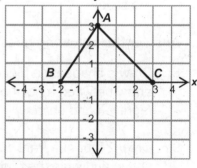

A (,) → A′ (,)
B (,) → B′ (,)
C (,) → C′ (,)

jump math
MULTIPLYING POTENTIAL.

Geometry 2

4. Reflect the set of points P, Q and R through the y-axis. Label the image point P', Q' and R':

HINT: The image of a point on the y-axis through the y-axis is the point itself.

a)
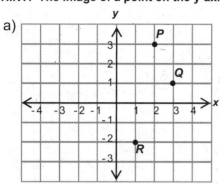

P (,) → P' (,)
Q (,) → Q' (,)
R (,) → R' (,)

b)
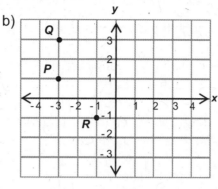

P (,) → P' (,)
Q (,) → Q' (,)
R (,) → R' (,)

c)
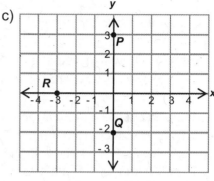

P (,) → P' (,)
Q (,) → Q' (,)
R (,) → R' (,)

5. Reflect the figure by first reflecting the points on the figure through the y-axis:

a)
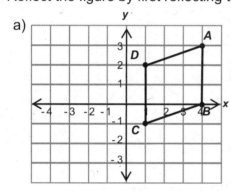

A (,) → A' (,)
B (,) → B' (,)
C (,) → C' (,)
D (,) → D' (,)

b)
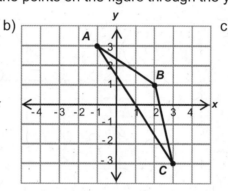

A (,) → A' (,)
B (,) → B' (,)
C (,) → C' (,)

c)
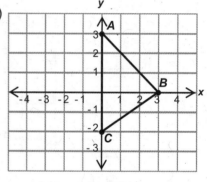

A (,) → A' (,)
B (,) → B' (,)
C (,) → C' (,)

6. a) Plot the points in the Cartesian plane:

A (3, 1)   B (–1, 1)   C (–3, 3)   D (1, 3)

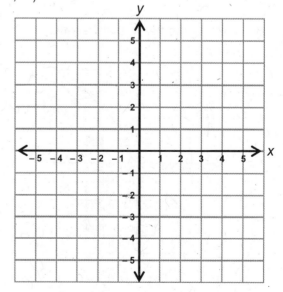

b) Reflect ABCD in the x-axis, label the image A'B'C'D'.

c) Write the coordinates:

A' (,)   B' (,)

C' (,)   D' (,)

d) Compare the area and the corresponding sides and angles of the figure and its image. Which of the following statements are true?

(i) Reflections create similar figures.

(ii) Reflections create congruent figures.

Line ℓ is an angle bisector of the axes and passes through the first and third quadrants. Notice that points (1, 1), (2, 2), (3, 3) … and (− 1, − 1), (− 2, − 2), (− 3, − 3) … are on line ℓ.

Example: Reflect point P(1, 3) through the mirror line ℓ.

Step 1: Draw a dotted line through point P perpendicular to line ℓ. Find the point where the dotted line meets ℓ and label it Q.

Step 2: Locate a point P′ on the dotted line such that P′ is the same distance from the mirror line ℓ as P: PQ = P′Q.

P′ is the image of P after reflecting through line ℓ.

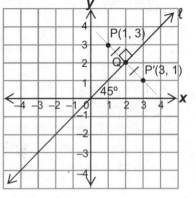

---

7. Reflect the set of points P, Q and R through the mirror line ℓ. Label the image points P′, Q′ and R′.

a)

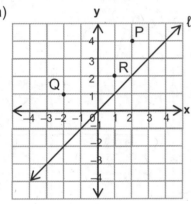

P (,) ⟶ P′ (,)

Q (,) ⟶ Q′ (,)

R (,) ⟶ R′ (,)

b)

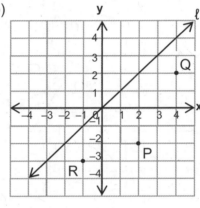

P (,) ⟶ P′ (,)

Q (,) ⟶ Q′ (,)

R (,) ⟶ R′ (,)

c)

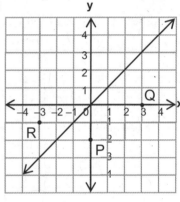

P (,) ⟶ P′ (,)

Q (,) ⟶ Q′ (,)

R (,) ⟶ R′ (,)

8. Reflect the figure by first reflecting the points through line ℓ:

a)

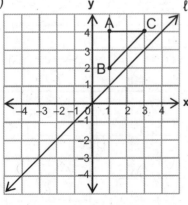

A′ (,) B′ (,) C′ (,)

b)

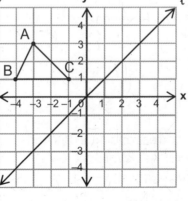

A′ (,) B′ (,) C′ (,)

c)

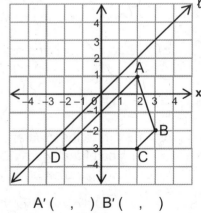

A′ (,) B′ (,)

C′ (,) D′ (,)

Example: Rotate the point P 90° clockwise about the origin. Label the image point P′:

Step 1
Join P and the origin:

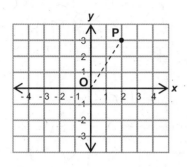

Step 2
Use your protractor to mark 90° clockwise:

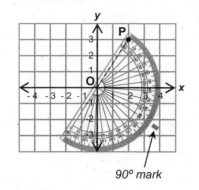

90° mark

Step 3
Use a ruler to draw a line from your mark to the origin. Then use a compass to find P′:

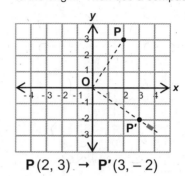

P(2, 3) → **P′**(3, − 2)

NOTE: Line Segments OP and OP′ must be the same length.

---

1. Locate point P (2, 3) in the Cartesian plane, then rotate P around the origin…

   a) 90° clockwise:

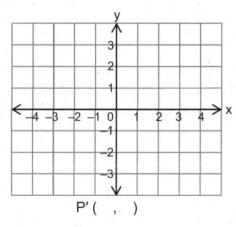

P′ (,   )

   b) 180° clockwise:

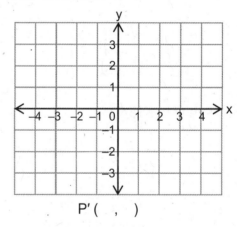

P′ (,   )

2. Locate point P (− 3, − 2) in the Cartesian plane, then rotate P around the origin:

   a) 90° counter-clockwise

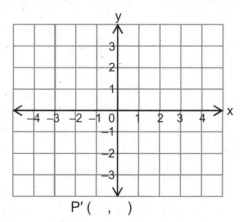

P′ (,   )

   b) 180° counter-clockwise

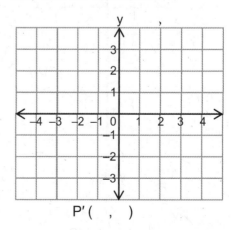

P′ (,   )

3. Compare the image of a) and b) in Question 2. What do you notice? Explain in your notebook.

4. Rotate the set of points P, Q and R around the origin. Label the image points P', Q' and R':

a) 90° counter-clockwise

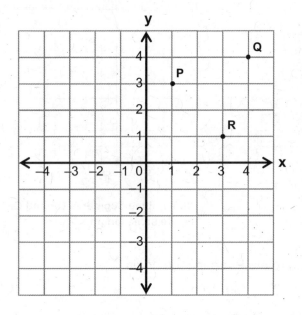

$$P (\quad,\quad) \longrightarrow P'(\quad,\quad)$$
$$Q (\quad,\quad) \longrightarrow Q'(\quad,\quad)$$
$$R (\quad,\quad) \longrightarrow R'(\quad,\quad)$$

b) 90° counter-clockwise

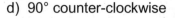

$$P (\quad,\quad) \longrightarrow P'(\quad,\quad)$$
$$Q (\quad,\quad) \longrightarrow Q'(\quad,\quad)$$
$$R (\quad,\quad) \longrightarrow R'(\quad,\quad)$$

c) 180° counter-clockwise

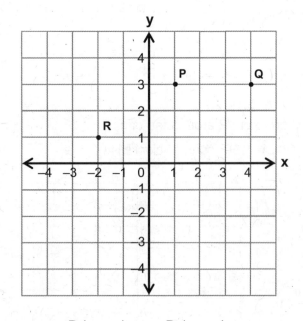

$$P (\quad,\quad) \longrightarrow P'(\quad,\quad)$$
$$Q (\quad,\quad) \longrightarrow Q'(\quad,\quad)$$
$$R (\quad,\quad) \longrightarrow R'(\quad,\quad)$$

d) 90° counter-clockwise

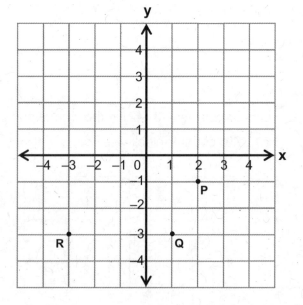

$$P (\quad,\quad) \longrightarrow P'(\quad,\quad)$$
$$Q (\quad,\quad) \longrightarrow Q'(\quad,\quad)$$
$$R (\quad,\quad) \longrightarrow R'(\quad,\quad)$$

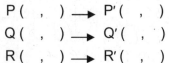

5. Rotate the figure around the origin by first rotating the points on the figure:

   a) 180° clockwise

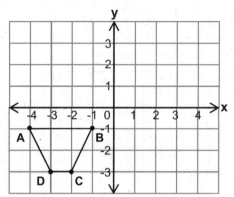

   b) 90° counter-clockwise

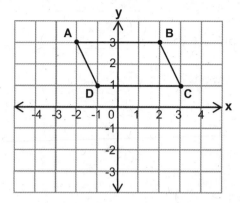

6. a) Write the coordinates of the points in 5 a) and b) in the table:

   b) What do you notice about the coordinates of the images A'B'C'D'?

Question	Points of original figures	Points of image figures
a)	A (,) B (,) C (,) D (,)	A' (,) B' (,) C' (,) D' (,)
b)	A (,) B (,) C (,) D (,)	A' (,) B' (,) C' (,) D' (,)

7. a) Plot the points in the Cartesian plane:

   A (–1, –2),   B (–1, –4),
   C (–3, –4),   D (–4, –2)

   b) Rotate ABCD 90° counter-clockwise, label the image A'B'C'D'.

   c) Find the coordinates

   A' (,)   B' (,)
   C' (,)   D' (,)

   d) Compare the area, corresponding sides and angles of the figure and its image. Which of the following statements are true?

   A. Rotations create similar figures.

   B. Rotations create congruent figures.

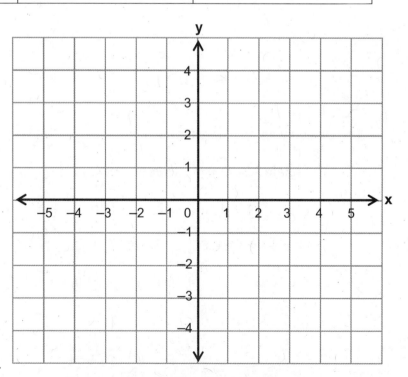

1. Which transformation changes triangle A into...

    a) triangle B? _____

    b) triangle C? _____

    c) triangle D? _____

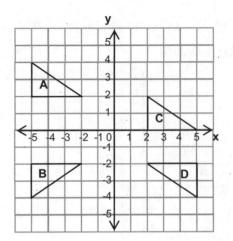

2. Draw a mirror line for the reflection.

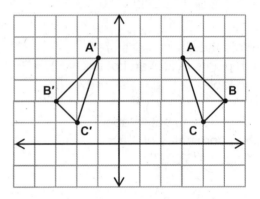

3. Identify the point F so that ΔDEF is congruent to ΔABC.

    NOTE: There are two possible answers.

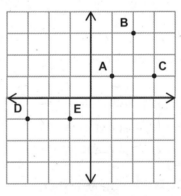

4. Design your own transformations.

    a) I rotate ABCD _____ degrees clockwise.

        A' (,) B' (,) C' (,) D' (,)

    b) I translate A'B'C'D' _____ units _____

        (up/down) and _____ units _____ (right/left).

        A" (,) B" (,) C" (,) D" (,)

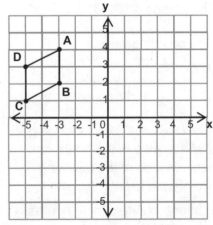

G8-38: Designs

Answer the questions below in your notebook.

1.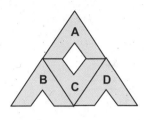

   a) Which transformation (slide, reflection or rotation) could you use to move shape A onto:

       (i) Shape B?   (ii) Shape C?   (iii) Shape D?

   b) Philip says: "I can move Shape C onto Shape B using a ½ turn and then a slide." Is he correct?

   c) Explain how you could move Shape C onto Shape D using a reflection and a slide.

2. The figure shows a section of the border of a picture frame:

   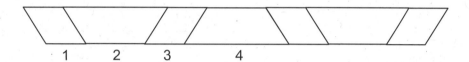

   a) Describe the design of the frame: (measure and describe each shape precisely).

   b) How many non-congruent shapes are used in the design?

   c) Describe a single transformation that will move the shape in position 1 to position 3.

   d) Describe a pair of transformations that will move the shape from position 2 to position 4.

3. Describe a sequence of transformations that would create each design (starting from the shaded figure):

   a) 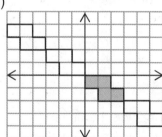   b) 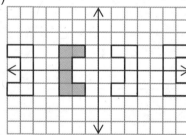   c)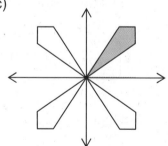

4. By shading squares, make a design that looks the same after a reflection in either mirror line.

   How many designs can you make?

   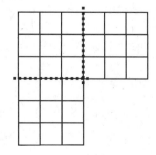

5. Describe the design by describing the shapes that make up the design and how they are arranged.

   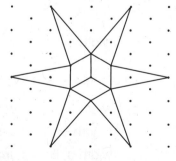

G8-39: Similarity

Two shapes are **similar** if they are the same shape (not necessarily the same size).

1. Copy ΔABC into the 2 cm grid. Label the vertices of the new triangle A', B' and C'.

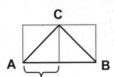

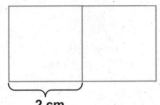

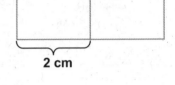

2 cm

a) Are ∠A and ∠A' the same size? How do you know?

_____

b) What is the measure of: ∠A_____ ∠A'_____ ∠B_____ ∠B'_____ ∠C_____ ∠C'_____

c) Are ΔABC and ΔA'B'C' the same shape? How do you know?

_____

2. Copy rectangle ABCD into the 3 cm grid.   Label the vertices A', B', C' and D'.

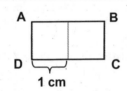

1 cm

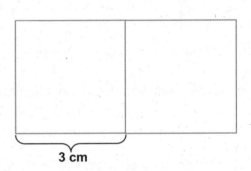

3 cm

What are the following ratios?

AB : A'B' = ___ : ___   BC : B'C' = ___ : ___   CD : C'D' = ___ : ___   DA : D'A' = ___ : ___

What can you say about the ratios of the corresponding sides in the two rectangles?

3. Rectangles A and B are similar. How can you find the length of B without a ruler?

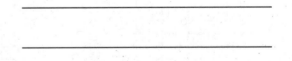

_____

_____

4. Rectangles A and B are similar. Find the length of B. (Don't forget to include the units!)

a) width of A: 2 cm   width of B: 4 cm   length of A: 5 cm   length of B: _____

b) width of A: 5 cm   width of B: 15 cm   length of A: 7 cm   length of B: _____

c) width of A: 1 cm   width of B: 9 cm   length of A: 9 cm   length of B: _____

5. Rectangle A and rectangle B are similar. Draw rectangle A on grid paper. Then draw B:

a) width of A: 1 unit
    length of A: 3 units
    width of B: 3 units

b) width of A: 2 unit
    length of A: 4 units
    width of B: 6 units

c) width of A: 5 units
    length of A: 8 units
    width of B: 10 units

Geometry 2

Answer the questions below in your notebook.

6. For each pair of rectangles below, say how you know the rectangles are similar or dissimilar.

a)

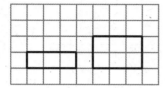

b)

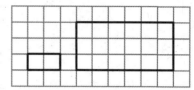

c)

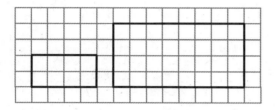

d)

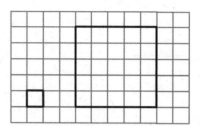

7. Draw a trapezoid similar to A with a base that is 2 times as long as the base of A. (A is 1 unit high. How high should the new figure be?)

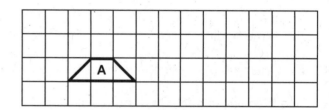

Which of these shapes are similar? How do you know?

8.

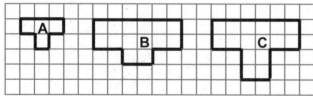

9. Which shapes are congruent? Which are similar?

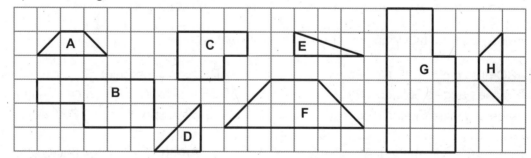

10. Draw a parallelogram on grid paper. Then, draw a similar parallelogram that is exactly twice as high as the first. Compare the areas of the figures.

11. Draw a right triangle on grid paper. Then, draw a similar triangle that is exactly three times as high as the first. Compare the areas of the figures.

12. Two triangles are similar if they have the <u>same</u> angles. Use a protractor and a ruler to construct two triangles that are similar but not congruent.

13. A square and a rectangle have the same angles. Are they similar? Explain.

14. Can a trapezoid and a square ever be similar? Explain.

1. △ABC and △DEF are similar:

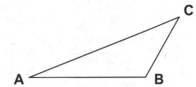

Measure all angles and all sides of the triangles:

AB = _____   ∠CAB = _____   DE = _____   ∠FDE = _____

BC = _____   ∠ABC = _____   EF = _____   ∠DEF = _____

CA = _____   ∠BCA = _____   FD = _____   ∠EFD = _____

Answer the remaining questions in your notebook.

2. Compare the corresponding angles in the triangles in Question 1 (i.e. ∠CAB and ∠FDE). Are they the same or different?

3. Find the ratio of all corresponding sides (i.e. AB and DE). What do you notice about the ratios?

4. The triangles in each question are similar. Find x and y:

   a)

   b)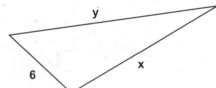

5. How could you prove two triangles are similar using only a protractor?

6. How could you prove two triangles are similar using only a ruler?

7. a) △ABC has angles 30°, 60°, 90°.
       △DEF has angles 35°, 55°, 90°.
       Are the triangles similar? Explain.

   b) △ABC has sides of length 2 cm, 4 cm, 7 cm.
       △DEF has sides 3 cm, 8 cm, 14 cm.
       Are the triangles similar? Explain.

8. Name two similar triangles in the diagram.
   How do you know they are similar?

9. Are the rectangles below similar?

10. What is the length of side x?

11. Are triangles ABC and CDE similar?
    How do you know?

A **dilatation** is a transformation that generates an image that is the same shape as the original figure.

Example A: Reduction

Example B: Enlargement

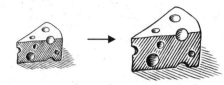

- -

1. For each dilatation, say whether the transformation is an enlargement, a reduction, or neither:

    a) _____

    b) _____

    c) _____

A dilatation is an **enlargement** when its scale factor is <u>greater than one</u>.

Examples of enlargements:

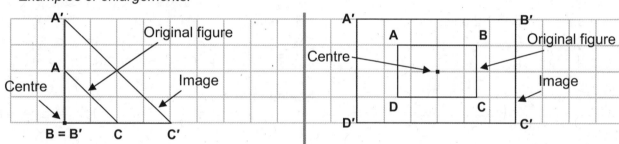

AB = 2 units   A'B' = 4 units

$\dfrac{A'B'}{AB} = \dfrac{4}{2} = 2$ $\dfrac{B'C'}{BC} = \dfrac{4}{2} = 2$ $\dfrac{A'C'}{AC} = 2$

Scale factor = 2

AB = 3 units   A'B' = 6 units

$\dfrac{A'B'}{AB} = \dfrac{6}{3} = 2$ $\dfrac{B'C'}{BC} = \dfrac{4}{2} = 2$ $\dfrac{C'D'}{CD} = 2$ $\dfrac{D'A'}{DA} = 2$

Scale factor = 2

---

2. Find the scale factor of the following enlargements:

    a)

    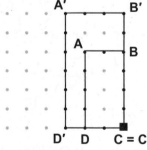

    $\dfrac{A'B'}{AB} = $ _____ =

    Scale factor =

    b)

    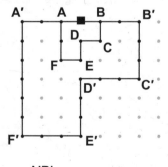

    $\dfrac{A'B'}{AB} = $ _____ =

    Scale factor =

    c)

    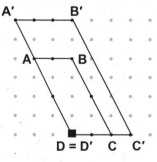

    $\dfrac{A'B'}{AB} = $ _____ =

    Scale factor =

d)
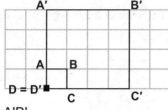

$$\frac{A'B'}{AB} = \underline{\quad\quad} =$$

Scale factor =

e)
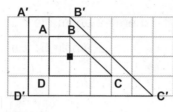

$$\frac{A'B'}{AB} = \underline{\quad\quad} =$$

Scale factor =

f)
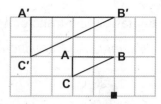

$$\frac{A'B'}{AB} = \underline{\quad\quad} =$$

Scale factor =

A dilatation is a **reduction** when its scale factor is <u>less than one</u>.

Examples of reductions:

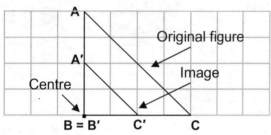

AB = 4 units   A'B' = 2 units

$$\frac{A'B'}{AB} = \frac{2}{4} = \frac{1}{2} \qquad \frac{B'C'}{BC} = \frac{2}{4} = \frac{1}{2} \qquad \frac{A'C'}{AC} = \frac{1}{2}$$

Scale factor = $\frac{1}{2}$

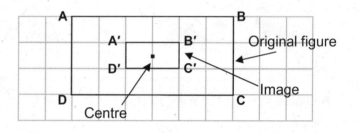

AB = 6 units   A'B' = 2 units

$$\frac{A'B'}{AB} = \frac{2}{6} = \frac{1}{3} \qquad \frac{B'C'}{BC} = \frac{1}{3} \qquad \frac{C'D'}{CD} = \frac{2}{6} = \frac{1}{3} \qquad \frac{A'D'}{AD} = \frac{1}{3}$$

Scale factor = $\frac{1}{3}$

---

3. Find the scale factor of the following reductions:

a)
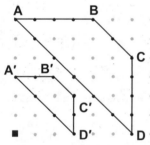

$$\frac{A'B'}{AB} = \underline{\quad\quad} =$$

Scale factor =

b)
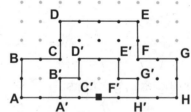

$$\frac{A'B'}{AB} = \underline{\quad\quad} =$$

Scale factor =

c)
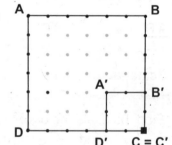

$$\frac{A'B'}{AB} = \underline{\quad\quad} =$$

Scale factor =

d)
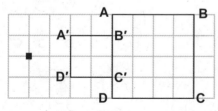

e)
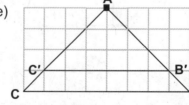

f)
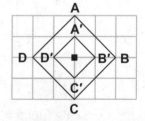

Example: Perform a dilatation, **scale factor = 2** in which the centre is at vertex D.

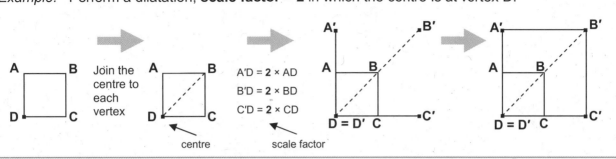

1. Perform the given enlargements where A is the centre, scale factor = 2:

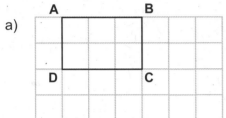

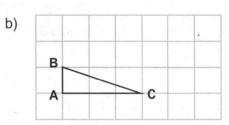

Example: Perform an enlargement, **scale factor = 2**, in which the centre is at the centre of ABCD.

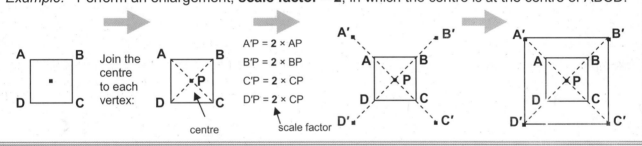

2. Perform the given enlargements where A is the centre, scale factor = 3:

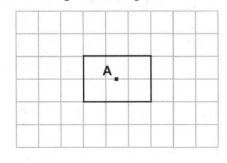

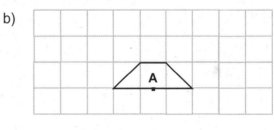

3. Copy the following shapes onto grid paper and perform the given enlargements:

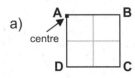

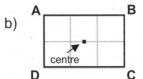

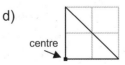

Scale factor = 2   Scale factor = 4   Scale factor = 3   Scale factor = 1.5

G8-43: Reductions

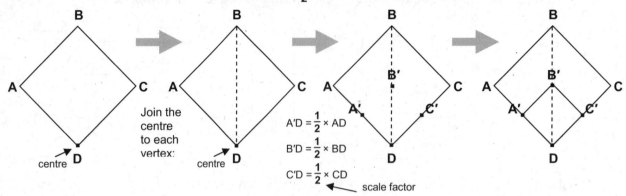

Example: Perform a reduction, **scale factor** = $\frac{1}{2}$, in which the centre is at D.

Join the centre to each vertex:

$A'D = \frac{1}{2} \times AD$

$B'D = \frac{1}{2} \times BD$

$C'D = \frac{1}{2} \times CD$ ← scale factor

1. Perform the given reduction using A as the centre. The scale factor = $\frac{1}{2}$:

a)

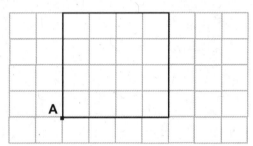

b)

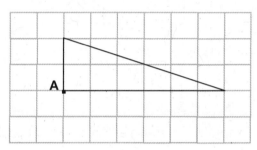

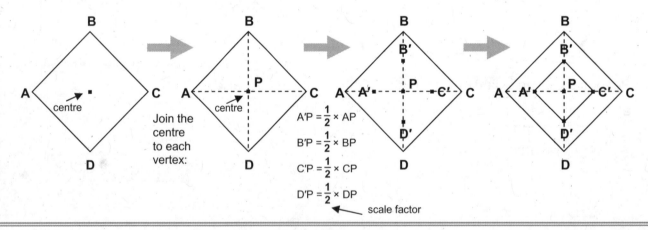

Example: Perform a reduction, **scale factor of** $\frac{1}{2}$, in which the centre is at the centre of ABCD.

Join the centre to each vertex:

$A'P = \frac{1}{2} \times AP$

$B'P = \frac{1}{2} \times BP$

$C'P = \frac{1}{2} \times CP$

$D'P = \frac{1}{2} \times DP$ ← scale factor

2. Perform the given reductions where A is the centre, scale factor = $\frac{1}{2}$:

a)

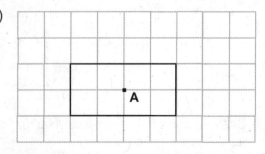

b)

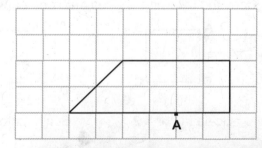

Geometry 2

G8-44: Enlargements (Advanced)

1. Start with a single pattern block triangle. Add shaded triangles to show what a scale factor = 2 enlargement (around a vertex) looks like. Repeat this step 3 times, shading in the added triangles. Then fill in the chart below:

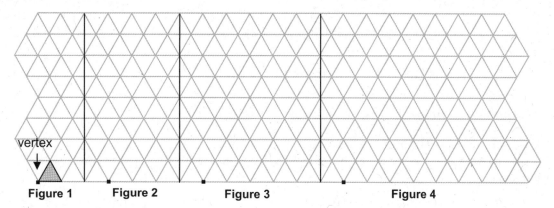

Figure 1   Figure 2   Figure 3   Figure 4

Figure	Side Length	Perimeter	Number of Unit Triangles
1	1 unit	3 units	1
2			
3			
4			

2. True or False: Enlargement. (Circle **True** or **False**.)

   a) The image side length **=** scale factor ×
   the corresponding side length of the original   **T** or **F**

   b) The image perimeter = scale factor ×
   the perimeter of the original image   **T** or **F**

   c) The image area = (scale factor)^2 × the original
   figure area   **T** or **F**

3. Repeat the exercise in Question 1 with the given shape below, scale factor = 2:

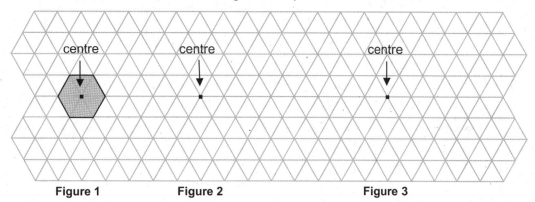

Figure 1   Figure 2   Figure 3

Figure	Side Length	Perimeter	Number of Unit Triangles
1	1 unit	6 units	6
2			
3			

4. True or False: Measure and compare the corresponding angles of the images and their original figures in Questions 1 and 3. (Circle **True** or **False**.)

   a) The corresponding angles of an image and
   its original figure are all equal.   **T** or **F**

   b) The corresponding sides of an image and
   its original figure are in the same ratio.   **T** or **F**

   c) Enlargements create similar figures.   **T** or **F**

G8-45: Pythagorean Theorem

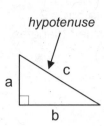

The longest side of a right-angled triangle is called the <u>hypotenuse</u>. Square the lengths of the two shortest sides of a right-angled triangle, then sum the results: $a^2 + b^2$. The sum will always equal the square of the length of the hypotenuse:

$$a^2 + b^2 = c^2$$

This is called the **Pythagorean Theorem**.

HINT:
If you know the length of the hypotenuse and one of the shorter sides, you can find the length of the other side.

$b^2 = c^2 - a^2$ or $a^2 = c^2 - b^2$

Answer the questions below in your notebook.

1. Use the Pythagorean Theorem to find the missing sides:

   HINT: **Start by deciding whether or not the unknown side is the hypotenuse. The hypotenuse is always opposite the right angle.**

   a)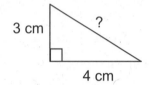

   b)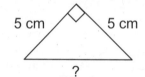

   c)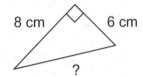

   d)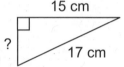

   e)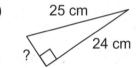

   f)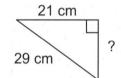

2.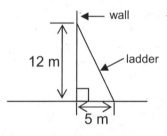

   How long is the ladder?

3.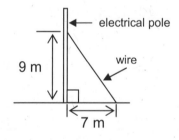

   How long is the wire?

4.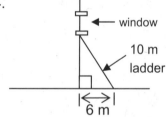

   How high is the window?

5.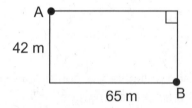

   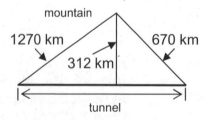

   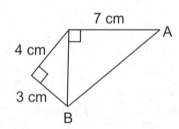

   a) What is the distance from A to B?

   b) How long is the tunnel?

   c) How long is AB?

6. Three nonzero whole numbers a, b, and c that satisfy $a^2 + b^2 = c^2$ are called a Pythagorean triple. Write down the first 15 perfect squares. How many Pythagorean triples can you find?

7. If you multiply or divide each number in a Pythagorean triple by the same number, the result is a Pythagorean triple. Make 3 Pythagorean triples using the numbers 6, 8 and 10.

 jump math
MULTIPLYING POTENTIAL

hypotenuse

c

b

a

The longest side of a right triangle (marked with a c) is called the **hypotenuse**. It is always opposite the right angle. The square of the length of the hypotenuse of a right-angled triangle is always equal to the sum of the squares of the other two sides:

$$c^2 = a^2 + b^2$$

In the exercise below you will prove this.

- -

Answer the questions below in your notebook.

1. On grid paper draw a right-angled triangle (choose a base and height that are whole numbers). Mark the hypotenuse with the letter c.

    Example:

    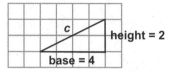

2. Draw a triangle that is congruent to the first triangle but is turned on its side as shown.

    NOTE: The angles marked x in both triangles are congruent, as are the angles marked y.

    Example:

    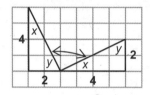

3. How do you know the angle marked with an arrow in Question 2 is 90°? Explain.

4. Place four congruent right-angled triangles as shown. How do you know the shaded figure is a square?

    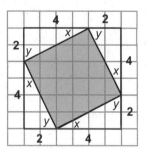

5. Write an expression for the area of the shaded square using the letter c, from Question 1.

6. The figure shows a different way to subdivide the large square. Write the area of each shaded square on the square:

    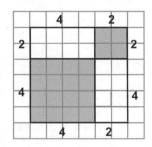

7. How do you know each of the 4 white triangles is congruent to each of the white triangles in Question 4?

    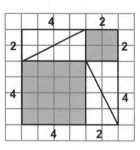

8. Look at the shaded squares in Questions 4 and 7. How do you know the area of the large shaded square in Question 4 is equal to the combined areas of the two shaded squares in Question 7?

9. How do you know $c^2 = 4^2 + 2^2$?

10. Repeat these exercises with several different right-angled triangles. Do you see why $c^2 = a^2 + b^2$?

Geometry 1

G8-47: Prisms and Pyramids

A **pyramid** has **one base**:

Example

NOTE: There is one exception – a triangular pyramid with congruent faces.

A **prism** has **two bases**:

Example

NOTE: There is one exception – a cube.

The base(s) are not always on the bottom or top of the shape. You can find the base by finding the face or faces that are different from the rest. However, if all the faces of a figure are congruent, *every face* is a base (as in a cube or a triangular pyramid).

---

1. <u>Shade</u> the base and <u>circle</u> the point of the following pyramids:

a)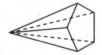
b)
c)
d)

e)
f)
g)
h)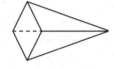

2. Shade the bases of these prisms:

a)
b)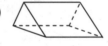
c)
d)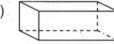

e)
f)
g)
h)

3. Shade the bases of the following figures:

a)
b)
c)
d)

e)
f)
g)
h)

i)
j)
k)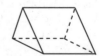
l)

jump math
MULTIPLYING POTENTIAL.

E Geometry 2

G8-48: Faces, Edges and Vertices

Faces of a 3-D shape are the flat surfaces of a shape, **edges** are where two faces meet and **vertices** are the points where three or more faces meet.

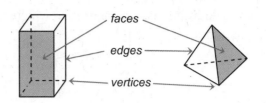

faces
edges
vertices

----

1.   Using a set of 3-D shapes for reference, fill in the first three rows of each chart. Then, using the patterns in the columns of the chart, fill in the fourth row:

a)

	Shape of Base	Number of...		
		...sides on the Base	...edges in the Pyramid	...vertices in the Pyramid
Triangular Pyramid				
Rectangular Pyramid				
Pentagonal Pyramid				
Hexagonal Pyramid				

b)

	Shape of Base	Number of...		
		...sides on the Base	...edges on the Prism	...vertices in the Prism
Triangular Prism				
Rectangular Prism				
Pentagonal Prism				
Hexagonal Prism				

Answer the following questions in your notebook.

2.   Describe any relationships you see in the columns of the charts in 1 a) and 1 b).

   EXAMPLE: What is the relationship between the number of sides in the base of the pyramid and the number of vertices (or the number of edges in the pyramid)? Answer the same question for a prism.

3.   How many edges and vertices would the following 3-D shapes have?
   a)   An octagonal pyramid (the base would have 8 sides).
   b)   An octagonal prism.

jump math
MULTIPLYING POTENTIAL

Geometry 2

A **Platonic solid** is a polyhedron in which all faces are congruent regular polygons. There are exactly five such solids:

| Tetrahedron | Cube | Octahedron | Dodecahedron | Icosahedron |

TEACHER: Give your students the nets for the Platonic solids from the Teacher's Guide.

4. Use the nets to construct the five platonic solids. Complete the table:

Polyhedron	Shape of the faces	Number of faces (F)	Number of vertices (V)	F + V	Number of edges (E)
Tetrahedron					
Cube					
Octahedron					
Dodecahedron					
Icosahedron					

5. Fill in the table based on the pictures given:

Polyhedron	Number of faces (F)	Number of vertices (V)	F + V	Number of edges (E)

6. Compare the sum of the number of faces and vertices to the number of edges in Questions 4 and 5. Use an equation to express what you found.

1. Name the object you could make if you assembled the shapes:

a)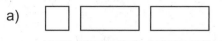

b)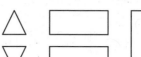

c)

_____ _____ _____

2.

A: B: C:

Shade the base of each shape above and then fill in the chart below:

	A	B	C
Number of sides on base			
Number of triangular faces			

What relationship do you see between the number of sides in the base and the number of triangular faces on the pyramid?

3.

A: B: C:

Shade the bases of each shape and then complete the chart below:

	A	B	C
Number of sides on base			
Number of (non-base) rectangular faces			

What relationship do you see between the number of sides in the base and the number of (non-base) rectangular faces on the prism?

4. How many of each type of face would you need to make the desired 3-D shape?

a)

b)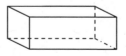

c)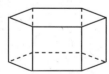

 = _____
 = _____

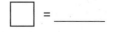 = _____
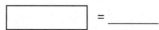 = _____

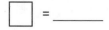 = _____
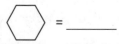 = _____

G8-50: 3-D Sketches

Steps to drawing a **cube** on isometric dots:

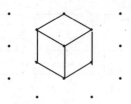

Step 1
Draw a square with 4 vertices at 4 different dots.

Step 2
Draw vertical lines at 3 vertices to touch the dots below.

Step 3
Join the vertices.

----

1. Draw the following figures constructed with the interlocking cubes on isometric dot paper. The first one has been started for you:

    a)

    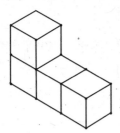

    b)

    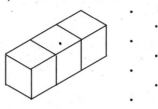

TEACHER:
Review top views of figures in section ME8-32. Your students will need a copy of the isometric dot paper from the Teacher's Guide.

2. Build a figure out of interlocking cubes having the following top views. Then copy the figures onto isometric dot paper:

    a)

2	2	1

    b)

3	2	1

    c)

2	1
2	1

    d)

3	1	1
2	1	

3. Draw a net for the triangular prism on isometric dot paper:

    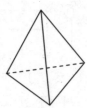

4. Draw a copy of the figure on isometric dot paper:

    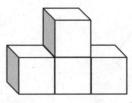

5. Create your own figure out of interlocking cubes and sketch it on isometric dot paper.